What People Are Saying About
Your School Rocks... So Tell People!

"For too long, the narrative of education has been shared mostly by people outside of education. That needs to—and can—change. In *Your School Rocks... So Tell People!*, the authors share great strategies on how to make a connection with your community, both locally and globally, and explain why that engagement is so important. This book beautifully guides you through the process of reaching people where they are, while helping you to develop the confidence and skill set to make this happen immediately. It is an easy, yet powerful read that can help you start making a difference today."

GEORGE COUROS, Division Principal and
Author of *The Innovator's Mindset*

"Educators are always hoping for more parent engagement. *Your School Rocks... So Tell People!* will help you turn that hope into reality. Ryan McLane and Eric Lowe provide simple instructions for using a variety of easy-to-use tools to engage the entire school community. Best of all, most take little time and are free! If you don't tell your school story, someone else will. This book will help you tell your story and keep your community informed and engaged in the great stuff you are doing in your building."

DR. JOE CLARK, Superintendent,
Nordonia Hill City Schools, Ohio

"Telling your story is such an important part of creating a positive culture that fosters learning. Eric and Ryan have methodically laid out simple steps to help make your school look like the gem of your community with a modicum of effort, which is why *Your School Rocks... So Tell People!* should be on every school leader's bookshelf."

JAY EITNER, National Speaker and Superintendent,
Waterford Township School District, New Jersey

"I have been an educator for the past thirty-four years, and the transformation that social media has brought to our school is the most exciting thing I have ever been part of. It has been an amazing and rewarding experience that has ultimately resulted in a school in which students are running to get in. Due to the efforts and commitment of Eric Lowe, our school is a wonderful place for students to learn, mature, and grow into productive citizens that care about their fellow man and their community. If you simply apply a few of the ideas in this book, you will see immediate results in your school's culture."

CONNIE SHIVE, Beaver Local Middle School Principal

"Mr. McLane allows parents to feel connected to school by engaging the kids in brief videos and sharing these videos on social media. My wife and I look forward to these videos to learn 'what's going on.' In addition, we enjoy the snapshots from the classroom with which we can engage our children at the dinner table with directed conversation and learn at a deeper level about what they're learning. We also see our kids' friends and the learning happening in other classrooms. These videos allow me, and parents like me, the opportunity to be involved in more meaningful ways than a typical newsletter or e-mail. We get to visually experience the events and learning alongside our children. It's an outstanding way to stay connected."

STEPHEN P. FUJII, Big Walnut Intermediate Parent

Your School
ROCKS...
So Tell People!

Passionately
Pitch and Promote the
Positives Happening on Your
Campus

Ryan McLane and Eric Lowe

Your School Rocks... So Tell People!
© 2015 by Ryan McLane and Eric Lowe

This book is available at special discounts when purchased in quantity for use as premiums, promotions, fundraising, and educational use. For inquiries and details, contact us: shelley@daveburgessconsulting.com.

Published by Dave Burgess Consulting, Inc.
San Diego, CA
http://daveburgessconsulting.com

Cover Design by Genesis Kohler
Editing and Interior Design by My Writers' Connection

Library of Congress Control Number: 2015956418
Paperback ISBN: 978-0-9861555-2-9
Ebook ISBN: 978-0-9861555-3-6

First Printing: December 2015

Contents

Chapter One

The Power to Connect

In the late 1990s, while preparing to become a teacher, I [Ryan] took a course in educational technology. One of my most vivid memories of that class was the professor telling us about a new technology—the LaserDisc™—that was going to revolutionize the way we presented material to our students.

As you may recall, the LaserDisc came and went, and no one would claim it revolutionized education. Even though the professor missed the mark with his prediction, he was wise enough to know that whether we are talking about pedagogy or the technology we use, educational practices are always evolving.

The same is true for how educators communicate. As Bob Dylan sang, "The times they are a changin.'"[1] We must reevaluate the traditional methods we use to communicate with our students, their families, and our communities because, quite frankly, there is a better way to communicate effectively. That way is social media.

We know what you are thinking: *Social media? Social media causes much of the drama I deal with in my classroom, school, and district on a daily basis. Why would we want to use it as a communication tool?*

We know that's what you are thinking because we felt the same way a few years ago. The potential negatives associated with social media kept us—and many other educators—from using it in our schools. Unfortunately, human nature focuses on negatives. (Just watch the local nightly news broadcast to see how it captures people's attention with stories of drama and trauma.) We thought of all the ways something could go wrong if we put our schools, teachers, and students on the World Wide Web for everyone to see. Any number of dangers and risks came to mind—as did the potential benefits. Despite our fears, it was difficult to deny the power of social media to connect people, disseminate information, and promote excellent ideas. We began asking questions. Could we, as educators, employ that power for good? Could we harness social media's power to show our school in a positive light—and maybe even impact human nature?

Two Challenges for Schools Today: Invisibility and Misinformation

One dilemma education faces today is invisibility. So many great things are happening in schools around the world that, for the most part, no one knows about. The traditional ways we communicate with families and our communities—newsletters, e-mails, and school websites—do not engage them the same way an Instagram or Facebook post does. The high-connection factor of social media provides students, teachers, and even administrators with a power prior generations did not have at their disposal. But with that power comes a lot of responsibility because a problem that's even more worrisome for schools than invisibility is misinformation.

Mr. Peabody's Apples (Callaway, 2003), a children's book written by Madonna, provides an excellent illustration of how misinformation can affect us. Mr. Peabody is an elementary school teacher and baseball coach whose reputation is ruined when his students see him taking an apple without paying as he walks past the fruit market. The children tell their parents and friends, and the rumor spreads that Mr. Peabody is a thief. Because of the coach's damaged reputation, only one boy shows up for the game the following week. The coach takes the boy to the fruit market, where the owner tells him that Mr. Peabody pays for his fruit at the beginning of the week so he can choose what he wants each day on his walk home.

The student who started the rumor, of course, feels awful and wants to help restore Mr. Peabody's ruined reputation. Mr. Peabody invites the student to the baseball field the next day and tells him to bring a pillow. At the top of the bleachers, Mr. Peabody has the boy cut open the pillow and let the feathers fly. He then tells the student to retrieve every single feather. Astonished, the student insists that finding every feather would be impossible. Mr. Peabody agrees and explains it would be equally impossible to find every single person who believes he is a thief.

Like the wind that carried those feathers away, social media has the ability to carry our message far and wide. These tools allow you to connect with people in ways that were never before possible and make an impact far beyond your school's doors. They also give you the capability to shape your school's reputation. But once you click "share," "comment," or "publish," you will never be able to find every single person who believes, retrieves, saves, and forwards what you've posted to represent you, your school, or your community. That means you need to think before you click and wisely use social media to spread a *positive message.*

Education stands at a fork in the road with regard to social media. As educators ourselves, we understand the ramifications of negative uses of social media. We have also seen its power to connect, engage and strengthen school communities. For example, I [Ryan] recently asked a prospective teacher to visit our school's Facebook, Twitter, and Instagram pages before coming to interview. Because of the variety of social media platforms we use to share our students' experiences, our prospective teachers have the opportunity to see the things happening in our school. I wanted her to see that the shared vision for our school is for students to learn *and* have fun. We do some unique things at Big Walnut Intermediate School—things worth sharing. But I also understand our school's environment is not every educator's cup of tea; frankly, our approach pushes some people outside their comfort zones. During the interview, I told her that if, based on what she had seen online, our school didn't appear to be a good fit for her, there would be no hard feelings. Instead, she simply asked, "When can I start?"

This same strategy can be used with students. When a student told me [Eric] that he was moving to Beaver Local Middle School from another district, I encouraged him to check out our school using Flipboard or Instagram so he could see what makes our school a little different. I explained that our goal is for students to want to run *into* our school, not out of it. Rather than simply telling him I think it's an excellent school, I asked him to check out the videos and photos and to judge for himself. By using social media to highlight the fun learning going on at our schools, we allow students, as well as teachers and our communities, to see what makes our schools a great place to be.

Throughout this book, we will discuss numerous ways you can use social media in your classroom, school, or district. We have both been administrators in schools that took the safe route and banned social media. But after exploring the topic and reflecting deeply, we each encouraged our school leaders to change course. The support and willingness of our central office staffs to try something new helped tremendously in the efforts to develop a positive and engaging online presence for each of our districts. Kent Polen (former superintendent of the Beaver Local Schools), Steve Mazzi (former superintendent of Big Walnut Local Schools), Angie Pollock (current superintendent of Big Walnut Local Schools), and Scott Hartley (superintendent of the North Fork Local Schools) were instrumental in their support and buy-in of the methods we proposed—methods we'll explain to you in this book. As a result, our schools' teachers, administrators, and students embraced the use of social media within our schools.

Our work in education has been greatly influenced by Dave Burgess and his book *Teach Like a PIRATE*. While we both tried to employ this philosophy as classroom teachers long before we knew about Dave and his book, we realized we were not employing it as administrators—at least not initially. Inspired by his message, we decided it was time to take back education and lead with our passion for kids and our belief that school should consist of learning *and* fun. Dave's philosophy that education raises human potential is one we take to heart. Social media allows us to reach out to students in their world. Connecting with them by meeting them where they are creates the foundation for a positive school culture. Some amazing things are happening in each of our schools, and social media is the tool we use to share these experiences with our students, their families, and the community.

This past year—my [Ryan] sixteenth in education—was the first year my own children attended schools in the district where I work. Now, anytime I happen to be in their building for a meeting, I take a few minutes and pop my head into their classrooms, just to see what they are doing. It always brings a smile to my face. I feel fortunate to have that opportunity. I know that ninety-nine percent of our students' families, like most parents, do not have the chance to see what their children are doing in the classroom on a regular basis. As a school, we can offer those families the next best thing: we can use social media to bring their children's experiences to them. From what Eric and I have seen, this is an avenue worth exploring because it creates connections between home and school, improves relationships between teachers and parents, and shows our students that we care about and are proud of their progress.

As we share what we've learned and experienced, we hope you'll see that incorporating social media into your messaging is not an all-or-none proposition. If you are considering implementing online communication in your classroom, school or district, go slowly. We will offer many different examples of how we have used social media in our schools, but it's important to note that we did not start to integrate them all at once. We began with just a few, using them until they became a part of our regular routines. As we learned about other types of social media, we evaluated how or if they fit into our communication plans. We gradually found more ways to use social media to share the phenomenal things happening in our schools and as a tool for two-way communication.

Our belief is that our purpose as educators is to raise human potential—not just test scores. Our commitment is to use the best available tools to strengthen that potential. Social media platforms, blogs, and online learning applications are a few tools we believe are essential for today's educators. We encourage you to take it slowly and to be consistent. Above all, start. Use the powerful tools at your disposal to help your students succeed.

Start the Social Media Conversation at Your School

This book will guide you through a variety of ways you can incorporate social media into your district, school, or even classroom. Please check with your building or district's decision makers before implementing any of these ideas. If your district currently prohibits the use of social media, use this book as a conversation starter to explore why those policies may be worth changing.

Getting Started

In the chapters that follow, we will share a few of the tools and social media platforms we recommend you consider for your classroom, school, and district. We'll explain each tool and its benefits and requirements. We'll also offer a number of examples of how we and other educators have successfully implemented these resources. Even if you are completely new to the social media game, you'll get a good feel for how to use each platform. Throughout the book, you will see QR codes that link to examples and how-to videos that will walk you through the process of setting up and using the different types of social media platforms.

If you are an experienced social media user, we hope the examples and stories provided in the following chapters will allow you to think of new or out-of-the-box ways to use the platforms with which you are already familiar. Whether you are a teacher, coach, building administrator, or central office administrator, we are confident you will find many ways to apply the examples to your needs.

Chapter Two
The Video Newsletter

Tools You'll Need:
iPad, iMovie, and YouTube

Average Time Commitment:
20 Minutes

reating a traditional Parent Newsletter is one task I [Ryan] never looked forward to. Keeping families informed of important upcoming events is vital and necessary, whether you are a teacher, principal, or a superintendent. But, when you take into account the hours it takes to create the content, format to make it visually appealing, edit, revise, print, and distribute, a traditional newsletter is a time-consuming process. This time could be spent on other tasks.

Even more frustrating than the time spent creating the newsletter was the reality that it wasn't being delivered. I constantly received parent phone calls and e-mails asking questions about information clearly included in the most recent newsletter. Newsletters collected in the bottom of student lockers, backpacks, and even on the hallway floor, which meant those paper newsletters were not making it home. Even when it did make it home, I had no way of knowing if the message was truly being delivered. Were our families engaged?

The final piece of evidence that proved the ineffectiveness of my paper newsletter was my own behavior as a parent. My daughter brought a paper newsletter home every Friday in her homework folder, but I did not read it on a regular basis. Was this my fault as a parent? To an extent, yes. However, just as teachers constantly seek more effective ways to engage struggling students, educators must do a better job of engaging students' families.

Here I was, a school principal—a person who truly values education and appreciated my daughter's principal taking the time to keep me informed of what was happening in her school—and I was not reading the paper newsletter. Worse, I also realized I was equally unlikely to read a digital version delivered via e-mail. The problem? I was not engaged. Like most parents, I was busy. Reading non-urgent correspondence from school didn't make the top of my list of things to do. I always thought I would get around to it, and, if something was really important, surely they'd send a note home from school.

Phil Griffin, a principal in Virginia, introduced me to the concept of a video newsletter when he tweeted a link to his own. I watched as Phil talked directly to the families of his students. The video showed photographs of what was happening in his school, and viewers got a glimpse of his personality. Once I viewed Phil's video newsletter, I knew it was a change I wanted—needed—to make. And now that I've made the change, I am a firm believer that trading a paper newsletter for a video newsletter is the greatest shift schools can make to move beyond communicating with families to truly engaging them with their stories.

Try Something New... And Remember to Smile

Using an iPad, iMovie, and YouTube, I created my first video newsletter. It was absolutely horrible! I was terrified of seeing myself on camera. I was monotone, lacked self-confidence, and showed little personality. When I uploaded the video to YouTube and sent the link to all of my students' families via e-mail, I was convinced it would be my first and *last* video newsletter.

What I didn't expect was the reaction of the students and their families. They absolutely loved it! Their comments poured in: "We love it," "Please keep doing this," "We actually watched it as a family after dinner," and finally, "Next time... smile."

The video newsletter appeared to solve the engagement problem, but I wasn't sure I could sustain it. Even if I smiled a bit more and showed some personality, I knew I could not sit in front of a camera and talk for two minutes per week and expect families to continue to be engaged. (There is a reason I am not a regular on television.) So I did what anyone else in my position would do: I found a student co-host and let him steal the show!

TIP

Keep your video newsletter under three minutes. Any longer and you'll lose your audience's attention.

My video newsletter accomplished two goals: First, it allowed me to communicate with families through a medium they actually used. Second, it enabled me to share the positive happenings in our school. But there were additional benefits I never anticipated. For example, student engagement increased. Recently, a parent told me his son routinely wakes up early on Saturday mornings to watch the latest video newsletter. The father applauded the school for finding a way to get his preteen son excited about school highlights on a Saturday morning. He was impressed that as a school, we had finally "figured *it* out"—the *it* being connecting with our students by engaging them.

Many parents have told me they watch the video newsletter as a family and then have conversations with their children about what is happening at school. Now, they're no longer having this conversation:

Parent: How was school today?

Student: Fine.

Parent: What did you do today?

Student: Nothing.

Instead, our families are having this conversation:

Student: Guess what we did in school today?

Parent: What?

Student: We had a video conference with a class from California.

Parent: Oh yeah?

Student: Yeah, I bet it will be on the video newsletter this week.

Another unintended benefit is that families and people in the community know who I am for the right reasons. Many parents have little interaction with the principal, and when they do, it is usually for a disciplinary reason.

The same is often true for teachers. When I was a classroom teacher of about 130 students, I usually did not have time, or make time, to engage in positive communication with families. If that's the situation you're in, you can be sure that your students' parents aren't getting the full story. If kids are telling their parents nothing special is happening at school, that is the parents' perception whether or not it is accurate. The video newsletter allows you to change that perception.

If kids are telling their parents nothing special is happening at school, that is the parents' perception whether or not it is accurate.

As a result of the video newsletter, our students' families feel as if they know me. When I talk directly to them in those last thirty seconds of each episode, they get to see my personality and recognize I am a human being—not just a figurehead at their child's school. The two or three minutes they see me each week have opened the door to meaningful relationships with them.

Nearly every time I meet with families, whether at the grocery store, a school function, or in my office to discuss a discipline issue concerning their child, a connection already exists. When I introduce myself, the family's response is usually something like, "I already know you from your videos." And because they have seen that I am committed to helping kids reach their potential, most discussions now focus on how we can work together to help their child, instead of debating whether or not their child is innocent.

How to Make Video Newsletters Work for You

What started with one fearful attempt is now part of my regular routine. I produce a two- to three-minute video newsletter every week. If anything is longer than three minutes, viewers become disinterested. Up until this school year, I did not have an assistant principal, so I created these videos myself, and it was not an overwhelming process. If you are fortunate enough to have someone assisting you, this process can be very efficient. Using a consistent format helps simplify the process. For me, that means each episode opens with quick introductions, and then we proclaim: "And here's what's going on!" Next, my student co-host and I banter back and forth for about fifteen seconds, and then the video transitions into photographs from the week. We highlight happenings in different classrooms. Either I or a student will record an audio to explain the pictures or video depicting the featured events. I conclude each episode by talking on camera, sharing important information about upcoming events.

Our Low-budget Production Studio

You may be thinking, "Well, that sounds great, but I certainly do not have time to do it." Actually, the video newsletter takes me significantly *less* time to create than my paper newsletters did. Additionally, it is low budget. We produce our video using an iPad and iMovie and then upload it to YouTube. I walk through our school and stop in classes almost every day, and I always carry my iPad with me. When I see something worth sharing with our community, I take a photograph or some video. This takes essentially no extra time since I am visiting classes anyway. During lunch or recess, I find my student co-host, and we record the opening video, propping up the iPad with some books on an old overhead projector cart and using the front-facing camera to record our segment. Seeing ourselves on the iPad allows us to get centered on camera. In the same manner, I use the front-facing camera to record my thirty-second information segment. You can record as many takes as you desire, but once you have done a few episodes, you will be able to record a segment in one or two takes.

TIP

Students make great co-hosts for video newsletters. Parents and classmates want to see kids in the spotlight!

Using iMovie I edit the video newsletter, a task that takes me no longer than fifteen minutes. Again, this is significantly less time than I devoted to the paper or e-mail newsletters. I can trim the video clips, arrange the photographs in the order I want, and add background music and voiceovers where appropriate. Involving the students as much as possible is my goal because doing so promotes greater family engagement. While parents like seeing the principal in the videos, they *love* seeing their own kids!

Once the video has been edited, it is uploaded to YouTube, and we share the link with families via e-mail, embed the video on our school web page, and post it to our school's Facebook and Twitter pages. On YouTube and Facebook, we can examine analytics that tell us how many views each video receives, which is typically several hundred each week. Before, I had no idea how many people were actually reading our paper or e-mail newsletters. Now I can see how many people are paying attention to our message.

Staying Connected— from Classroom Teacher to Superintendent

Video newsletters can be a great way for teachers to engage families as well. Rather than focusing on school news, teachers can use this tool to highlight how students achieved different learning objectives for the week and what the kids can expect for the upcoming week. I guarantee, as a parent, I would be watching that—especially if the kids help host the newsletter!

Jeremy Evans, a middle school teacher in Dover, Ohio, began using video newsletters this past school year to connect with his students and their families. He enlisted the help of his students to generate ideas for each episode and to produce the video as well. Jeremy told me that the kids loved seeing the video newsletters and replayed them multiple times, taking pride in seeing pictures of their work. One could only wonder if seeing their work promoted on video might motivate students to produce better quality work in hopes of having it featured on the next episode.

This school year, Jeremy is publishing his video newsletter on a biweekly basis. In an effort to make sure students' families see the video, he is using Remind (formerly Remind101) to push out the link to the video newsletters. Remind (Remind.com) is an app that families sign up for to receive text message reminders from their schools. The app is free for teachers and does not give recipients your cell phone number. Jeremy only uses Remind to send the video newsletter links to parents, so they know the alert indicates something they look forward to each week.

Jeremy is an example of a teacher who applies the philosophy of continual improvement to communicating with his students' families. His video newsletters have been very well received by his students' families because he constantly looks for ways to improve and to ensure they receive his messages.

My co-author Eric is doing this exact thing at Beaver Local Middle School. Recently promoted from assistant principal to principal, Eric implemented the video newsletter this school year. He is new to his position, and his school is moving to a new K-12 building, so there is much to share. Eric sees two primary benefits of the video newsletter. First, he can highlight upcoming events and news and also film and discuss various aspects of the school to assist in the transition to the new building. This informs the community about the different components of the new setting. Second, the video newsletter helps parents and community members get to know him in a fun, engaging manner on a weekly basis.

District administrators can also use video newsletters to showcase to the community what is happening in their schools. Due to the success of the video newsletter at Big Walnut Intermediate School, Assistant Superintendent Angie Pollock began creating a district-level video newsletter for the Big Walnut Local School District. In addition to giving her the ability to share all the great things happening in schools around our district, people got to know her through the videos. Another benefit of using these at a district level is your teachers will see what is happening in other classrooms around the district and perhaps be motivated to step up their game. In the end, the kids win.

One final story about our video newsletter: I typically release the video newsletter on Fridays, but when we were scheduled for parent-teacher conferences, I thought it might be a chance to see what actually happened when I sent the newsletter. I distributed the link one evening while parents were waiting to meet with the teachers. Within minutes, I witnessed multiple parents watching the video newsletter on their phones as they stood in the hallways. I doubt that instant response ever happened with my e-mail newsletters, which would have been longer, less engaging, and more difficult to read on a smartphone. That "gotta watch it now" mentality is part of what makes video newsletters one of the most valuable shifts I have made in our school's communication efforts.

Most parents want to know what's going on at their child's school. They care. They *want* to be informed. But, just like you and me, they are busy. Video newsletters are one way to connect with and engage in a format they're already comfortable using. And with fewer hours and less money invested in each distribution, they are a great place to start if you want to improve your communication with students, teachers, and families.

**Watch a sample
Video Newsletter.**

**Need some help
getting started?
Watch this video tutorial.**

Tips for Making a Video Newsletter

- Video newsletters take less time to produce than traditional newsletters.

- Keep it under three minutes in length to hold viewers' attention.

- Get students involved as much as possible.

- Upload or link it to multiple platforms (YouTube, Facebook, Twitter, school website).

- Video newsletters are not just for principals. They are great for superintendents, teachers, and athletic directors.

Chapter Three

iMovie Trailers

Tools You'll Need:
Smartphone or tablet, Macbook or Mac desktop, iMovie, and YouTube

Average Time Commitment:
10 Minutes

Sometimes just a few extra minutes of effort can make an unbelievable difference in the attitudes of students and parents. We've discovered that creating a short video trailer—like a movie preview you would see at the theater—is a quick, easy way to build excitement for anything from the big game against the crosstown rival to the social studies lesson about Ellis Island.

Choose Your Claim to Fame

In 2013, I[Ryan] was the principal of a small junior high school in the North Fork Local School District in Utica, Ohio, with about 280 students in grades seven and eight. Approximately 50 percent of the students were on free or reduced lunch, and our test scores had been near the lowest in the surrounding area. During my first year as principal, we placed a large focus on improving student test scores, assessing kids on an ongoing basis, altering instruction, providing remediation where necessary—and our scores soared! While some would say we began to teach to the test, I would argue we did much more than that to turn our scores around. What was the bottom line? Improving our state test scores was our claim to fame.

We went from the bottom of the county in all subject areas to near the top in all areas. Our teachers felt on top of the world—and so did I! But here is the irony: while this had been our biggest focus and what we were most proud of, no one in the community seemed to care. Not a single person ever mentioned our improved tests scores. But as I reflected back, I could not recall anyone mentioning the scores when they were poor either. Surely being a student and an educator had to have more meaning than tests.

Toward the end of the next school year, as our test scores continued to rise, we did something unique. On May 22, 2013, we held the world's first Teach like a Pirate (TLAP) Day, based on Dave Burgess' book *Teach Like A PIRATE*. One of the essential questions Dave asks is, "If your kids did not have to be there, would you be teaching to an empty room?"[1] We decided to put that question to the test.

After checking in with their homeroom for attendance, students were allowed to go to any classes they wanted on TLAP Day; they did not have to follow their normal schedule. Students received a guidebook the day before, which included descriptions of each experience available that day.

No one at our school had ever done TLAP Day. In fact, most of my teachers had not even read the book, and our students certainly did not know anything about it. But I knew TLAP Day had the potential to be the most amazing academic day of our students' lives, and I wanted to build up the anticipation and get everyone—students, teachers, *and* families—excited about the day.

Create Excitement and Anticipation

We created a short video trailer from iMovie to promote TLAP Day. Not only did we share this video with our students during home room, but we also shared it on our school's Facebook page, so our families and the community could learn about the day.

TLAP Day Video Trailer

You may be thinking, "TLAP Day sounds like a disaster waiting to happen," and you would not be alone. But it was not. Honestly, it was the most amazing day of school I had ever seen—not just as a principal or teacher, but even as a student. I was jealous of what these kids got to experience. Our kids were excited to come to school on TLAP Day. Our attendance rate was 99 percent, and there was not a single discipline issue that day. Our kids were literally running *to* the next class because the day was awesome.

The following year, I changed jobs and became the principal at Big Walnut Intermediate (BWI). The BWI students had an equally amazing experience when it hosted a TLAP Day in May of 2014. At both schools, teachers created phenomenal learning experiences for

Our kids were literally running *to* the next class because the day was awesome.

students. For example, during our inaugural TLAP Day, seventh-grade science teacher Darin Prince created a class focused on science experiments you could do at home. I had never seen kids so engaged. At Big Walnut, fifth-grade math teacher Karen Bodker created an activity similar to the television show *The Amazing Race* during which students traveled to different locations and solved math problems in order to receive their next clue. However, these were not your ordinary math problems. At one location students found a bicycle tire and had to calculate its circumference. Once they determined the correct answer, they received their next clue and were off to solve the next problem. Kids were *racing* to solve math problems!

TLAP Day sold itself to the kids once it began. But the video trailer is what initially hooked them—convincing them well in advance that it was the one day of school they absolutely did not want to miss.

TIP

Video trailers can be used to promote special activities, visiting speakers, field trips, concerts, plays, or sporting events.

Last year I [Eric] was fortunate to visit Big Walnut for its inaugural TLAP Day. Immediately, I knew we had to hold a TLAP Day at Beaver Local. We mimicked many of the strategies Ryan had successfully implemented, including the use of an iMovie trailer to generate excitement among staff and students. The video was highlighted as part of our opening day of school with the words "Coming Soon." Staff and students regularly asked when Teach like a Pirate Day was going to be—even during a trying year with state testing changes causing a great deal of stress. Once we settled on a date later in the year, the video was posted to YouTube and other social media outlets and was shown at school to continue to increase students' excitement about this great learning opportunity.

Our TLAP Day was scheduled on a snow make-up day which often equates with high absenteeism. But we had *full* classes—students ran from class to class and our teachers were excited about this fun, interactive day of learning.

Just Add Photos—and Hook Your Students!

A variety of methods and tools are available to create a video trailer. iMovie is the most time-efficient tool and is available on many handheld devices. The MacBook and desktop versions have even more bells and whistles, including several preloaded themes to help you customize your video trailer. All you need to do is add photographs or videos and titles, and you can build excitement and hook your students!

TIP

iMovie templates make it simple to create professional-looking video clips.

Using iMovie to create a movie trailer does not take a great deal of time. And the result can be a highly engaging video that excites your target audience about any upcoming event, no matter how big or small.

Need some help getting started? Watch this video tutorial

Tips for Making an iMovie Trailer

- Collect the appropriate digital photos or video clips.

- Select the trailer theme that is the most appropriate for the event you are promoting.

- Choose the photos and videos that will make your movie trailer the most appealing.

- Change the titles in the iMovie trailer maker to fit your needs.

Chapter Four

iMovie Movies

Tools You'll Need:
iPad and iMovie App

Average Time Commitment:
**10-20 Minutes
(depending on the length)**

The iMovie application is a great PR tool you can use to build rapport with your school community and highlight school events. And, bonus, it is extremely inexpensive. Unlike the iMovie trailer option, the iMovie movie feature does not have set storyboards, which allows you the freedom to create the kind of video you want. Do not let the lack of pre-set storyboards scare you; the app is still very user-friendly. The program allows you to gather photos and videos from the year and sync music to create an action-packed video everyone can enjoy, for free. You'll find that these movies serve as keepsakes for students and their families, and they can also create excitement about school. iMovie allows you to easily slot images into the audio to highlight special events and moments from the school year. Administrators can use these for year-end functions like grade recognition or graduation, and teachers can use them to highlight class experiences from the year or wrap up a unit or hands-on activity.

Send out a link to your school's year-end movie in your video newsletter.

Showcase Student Experiences

For the past two years at Beaver Local Middle School, we have used iMovie to create videos to highlight our eighth grade students' year. We show them prior to the recognition program and post them to YouTube. The movies are about ten minutes long and are set to musical themes, which tie into our school year and highlight the great successes and memories students have created. We include many images of students engaged in group activities to ensure all students are featured in the videos. We post shortened versions of these on Twitter and Instagram or via links so our students and families can access them. Each year, many ask to purchase the movie and are surprised to learn it is free on YouTube.

Movies serve as keepsakes for students and their families and can create excitement about school.

Year-End Movie

Currently, a couple of our classroom teachers are creating year-end movies to showcase their classes' learning experiences. These videos communicate to students that we value their efforts and also highlight the growth we have shared with each other over the year. What's especially nice is they can be uploaded, viewed, and reflected on in the future.

Joe Evener, a fifth-grade language arts and social studies teacher at Big Walnut Intermediate, is a great example of a classroom teacher employing this technique in the classroom. For the past two years, Joe has had his students assist him in creating a video for the following year's class. He uses the video to preview the exciting things the new kids will get to experience in his class. His current students give the new students advice about how to be successful in Mr. Evener's class and how they can maximize their learning experience. What a great way for the new students and their families to get to know about their teacher and his class! Once he uploads the video to YouTube, he also distributes it to the new families through e-mail and places a link on his class web page.

Welcome to the Class

Launch the School Year and Create Excitement

iMovie movies can be used in other great ways as well. For example, they can serve as a launching pad to the school year. Each of the past three years, I [Eric] have created iMovie movies to use with both our staff and students as we open school. We incorporate messages for our students about character and encourage them to be the best people they can be each day at Beaver Local Middle School. We also use these video messages with our staff to generate excitement and to remind them of our philosophy to make school about learning *and* fun as we focus on the most important thing: our students.

A Tour of Your New School

At both of our schools, we use these beginning-of-the-year movies to put our students at ease. Our students transition to our campuses from multiple elementary schools, gathered together for the first time in one school in the district. Some of them are nervous about attending a larger school with students they don't know and procedures with which they are not familiar. We do not want them to be nervous; we want them to be excited. We want them to see they are about to embark on an unbelievable journey. One way we attempt to accomplish this is by creating a movie to show how students from different elementary schools come together to create one school.

"All About the Snow"

This past year, we both had students create snow-day videos using iMovie. What made these videos fun was that they involved both students and administrators and were not released until the first snow day. The students at Beaver Local entirely choreographed and created their "All About the Snow" video as a parody of Meghan Trainor's song *All About That Bass*. When school was canceled for snow, the video was posted to YouTube, Twitter, and Instagram, and was a huge success! To announce their first snow day, the kids at Big Walnut Intermediate created a parody of Taylor Swift's *Shake It Off* and called it "We're Taking Off." Students were excited about the debut release of their movies as school was canceled for the first time of the season, highlighting the culture and environment we are trying to create in our schools—one which students are excited to be a part of.

TIP

Don't stress out! Movies don't have to be feature-length productions. Think short. Two to twenty minutes is perfect.

Promote Character Development

This past year, I [Eric] used iMovies with students at career days and other classroom opportunities. The movies conveyed messages related to character development, optimism, followers and leaders, and about using social media in a responsible manner—themes we wanted to emphasize. "Each person matters" was the theme at Beaver Local Middle School, and we focused on the fact that a simple word or action could make a positive impact on others. As I taught a mini-lesson or made points relevant to our discussion, I showed iMovies I'd created to engage the students and asked them to choose a couple of their favorite quotes from the short movie. At the end, we discussed some of their favorites. Just as teachers use exit tickets at the end of class to check for understanding, we had students post messages on "exit" character boards to serve as a wrap-up. At the same time, students were encouraged to use their devices to find quotes of their own to add to our board or post to social media using the #blmsyoumatter hashtag. The hashtag allowed us to gather all of the tweets and Instagram messages so we could use them the following day as a discussion platform. Students were also permitted to use e-mail if they preferred.

TIP

Meeting students and parents where they are requires flexibility on your part, but the payoff is an engaged community.

Students were excited to participate in this format. They engaged in collaborative discussions about the quotes and connected those powerful words to ways in which they could impact our school. The students even asked if they could add more items to our character "exit" board. They also looked for ways to show others that "you matter."

Two of my students even created their own movies, modeled after ones we used in class which featured their own messages. They were so excited about what they had learned about character development and how the right character traits can make a positive impact on their school on a daily basis that they decided to make their own movie as a way to share what they had learned.

As you can see, you can use the iMovie application in multiple ways to share what is happening in your school with your stake-holders and to get them *excited* about it. Videos—whether they are two or twenty minutes long—are very powerful tools because the viewer actually *sees* what is happening. And as they say, "seeing is believing."

Need some help getting started? Watch this video tutorial

Tips for Making an iMovie Movie

- Use iMovies to generate excitement among staff and students for upcoming events.

- The iMovie app can be used to create powerful videos for instruction or to showcase student experiences.

- Educators can use iMovies with students to highlight classroom events, and students can easily create their own iMovies.

Chapter Five

Facebook

Tools You'll Need:
Smartphone, tablet, or computer, and Facebook app or Facebook website

Average Time Commitment:
1 Minute per post

F*acebook.* We know what you are thinking because we used to feel the same way. If you had told either of us four years ago that we would write about why schools should use Facebook, we would have laughed uncontrollably. Early in our school administration careers, we saw very little positive use of social media, especially when it came to Facebook. It seemed that most of the student drama in middle school originated from students' use of Facebook, either comments or photos posted, or something else related to Facebook.

Similar to the way I [Ryan] learned about the video newsletter, another principal from Virginia, Dr. Travis Burns, opened my eyes to how a school could use Facebook for a variety of positive purposes. Dr. Burns prompted me to examine whether it was the tool—or the way people *used* the tool—that caused the drama. If Facebook was not the problem, could we influence students and families to use it in a positive manner? While I did not know initially if we would ultimately adopt using Facebook, we were committed to giving it a shot. Why? Because a lot of our parents used Facebook, we wondered if this platform could be an effective way to reach them. Dr. Burns and his school appeared to be having success with it, so we decided to see for ourselves.

Go Where Your Audience Is

According to a 2015 study conducted by the Pew Research Center, 75 percent of parents use social media. Of all parents who use the Internet, 74 percent of them use Facebook. Finally, of those parents who use Facebook, 75 percent of them use it daily.[1] If we as educators refuse to examine how we can harness the power of Facebook for positive purposes, we are missing an *incredible* opportunity to connect with our students' families.

The myth is that teens are no longer using Facebook. While it may seem like more teens have migrated away from Facebook to other social media platforms in recent years, the statistics do not support that. Seventy-one percent of American teens have a Facebook account and 41 percent say the platform is the one they use the most, more than doubling the next most popular platform, Instagram.[2]

Nevertheless, adults are the demographic that has been growing most in recent years in terms of Facebook use. Parents, aunts, uncles,

If you want to reach your audience, it makes sense to go where they are.

and grandparents—a large part of the audience schools need to reach—all appear to be flocking to it. If we are not targeting them with our communication, we certainly should be. Who better to share the exciting news about what is happening in our schools than with Grandma Rita or dear Aunt Patty? Looking at even the worst statistical scenario,

Facebook enables us to communicate with about 74 percent of our families. Can you remember a time and place where you have had nearly 74 percent of your key stakeholders gathered in any one place? If you want to reach your audience, it makes sense to go where they are—especially when so many of them can be found in one location.

My first time to use a school Facebook page was at Utica Junior High School. Our use of Facebook was as conservative as possible. We did not post close-up pictures of students, and we never used students' names. We would post photographs of interesting classroom activities but made sure that the photographs were shot from the rear of the classroom. Despite this conservative strategy, the families of our students absolutely loved it. How did we know? They told us!

Facebook 101 for Educators

Due to this success, I brought Facebook communication with me to Big Walnut Intermediate School. At Big Walnut, we are less conservative with our use of Facebook. After many conversations with our families and community members, we determined it wasn't necessary to be so restrictive. We routinely post photographs of students and their faces in candid shots, as well as posed photos, for recognition of an achievement, such as Student of the Month or State Science Qualifier. Facebook has been a great tool to share positive school happenings and to keep parents updated with important information. All seven of the schools in the Big Walnut Local School District have a Facebook page. My school's Facebook page currently has 584 likes, so I know when we share information, a photograph, or a video, 584 people have that information on their Facebook newsfeed. If they decide something is worth "liking" or sharing, our reach becomes far greater.

What about families who do not want their child's image to be used on Facebook? Great question! We simply know who those students are, and we do not use their images on social media. While it might sound like a logistical nightmare to keep track of which students can and cannot be on social media, that has not been our experience. This past school year, we had six families who chose to "opt out" of having their children's photographs posted to social media. Of those six, four of them did not realize what they had "opted out" of and opted back in. At the beginning of each school year, we provide a straightforward explanation of how we use social media. We want our families to feel comfortable and confident with this aspect of our communication. And we respect the decisions of families who "opt out," never putting them in a position where they have to defend or explain that decision. In the end, we had permission to use the images of 518 of our 520 students, so it was pretty easy to remember who those two were and not post their photographs.

Facebook offers a couple of setup options for your page. You can set up a personal page, which is likely what you have for your Facebook account. The other option is to create a business or organization page, which doesn't require "friend requests." With a personal Facebook page, users accept one another's friend requests, and each user can see almost everything on the other person's Facebook account. As much as some families may want to see what is happening with their child's education via the school's Facebook page, they may not want their child's principal to see their personal Facebook posts.

TIP

Create a Facebook Page for your school or classroom and then choose the privacy setting that's right for your community.

By creating our school's Facebook page as a business/organization page, a parent can "like" our page—which gives them access to our content—without giving the school access to see their personal pages or posts. To be completely honest, I do not want to see what our parents are posting on their personal Facebook pages, and I believe they feel comfort knowing I *cannot* see it.

What About Allowing Comments?

Another choice you have when creating your Facebook page is whether or not to allow comments. At this point, you may figure you can stop reading this paragraph because there is absolutely no way we would tell you to allow comments. No good reason exists for ever allowing comments, right? Well, actually, we *do* allow comments on our school Facebook pages. Yes, you read that correctly: we allow comments. Let us explain.

If you are worried about people posting negative comments on your school's Facebook page, *not* allowing comments is *not* stopping those conversations from happening. However, not allowing comments *is* preventing you from knowing about them. Wouldn't we rather know about someone's dissatisfaction than pretend it is not happening? Sometimes a family's complaint has merit and is based on something I was unaware of. Sometimes a family's complaint is completely wrong and based entirely on false information. Either way, because we allow comments, I am now aware of the situation and can work to find a solution to the problem. But I do *not* get into a Facebook "comment war." I pick up the phone and call the family personally.

I have used a school Facebook page for about three years, and I can count on one hand the number of times there has been a negative comment posted there. Since we keep *our* posts positive, parents tend to be positive as well. When you use Facebook to address negative issues, such as dress code or students being dropped off too early in the morning, you are opening the door for negativity. Those issues are certainly worth addressing with parents, but Facebook is not the appropriate platform for those conversations.

TIP

Facebook allows you to choose settings that ban profanity in comments and require that posts (not comments) are approved before they are visible on your page.

Eric discovered another reason to allow comments when his district was trying to pass a bond issue to build a new K-12 building. The Beaver Local School District's Facebook page was originally set up to assist with the levy campaign. In Ohio, if a school district needs additional taxpayer money, a levy measure can be put on the election ballot for voters to approve or reject. (My father, a long-time educator, finds this process difficult to fathom. He lives in Pennsylvania where, if a school district decides it needs additional money, the school board can raise residents' taxes without their consent. He finds it hard to believe anyone would vote in favor of increasing his own taxes. Getting these tax increases is not an easy endeavor, and, sadly, due to the school funding policy in Ohio, many districts need to convince voters to do the impossible—approve the increase to their taxes.)

The superintendent at the time, Kent Polen, helped manage the school's Facebook page as he found it useful for getting information to voters in a quick, efficient manner. This also allowed him to ensure the Beaver Local community had current information along with

**Beaver Local
Facebook Page**

**Big Walnut Intermediate
Facebook Page**

FAQs and more updates than you would find through mail. In addition to using the page to post locations of town hall meetings, Q&A sessions, and open houses, it was also a place where he could respond to comments and questions posted by voters.

The bond was placed on the ballot and passed successfully for the first time in nine years for a variety of reasons, including a great support group who helped to organize the campaign. Facebook also played a role in the bond's success. The social media platform made it possible to make information available to a large segment of voters.

Likewise, the page allowed the district to keep the community informed with updates about the construction of the new school and provided a venue for responding to questions and concerns about many items related to the new building. One valuable feature of Facebook is that you can respond to concerns of your community members, clarify incorrect information, and ensure inaccurate perceptions do not become someone's reality. In the spring of 2015, the Big Walnut Local School District asked its residents to approve a five-year renewal of a tax increase that was originally passed in 2010. While this levy would not *raise* the taxes of its residents, voters could vote "no" and see their tax payments reduced to what they were paying prior to 2010. The result? Residents overwhelmingly voted "yes"—to continue paying the higher tax rate originally passed in 2010. Once again, social media, especially Facebook, helped the school district keep the community informed and engaged.

Rather than simply campaigning in the months leading up to the election, we had been consistently informing the community of the great happenings in the school. Nearly every day for the past two years, families of our students and other members of the community were reading and seeing what was happening in our schools. Because of that, I believe our campaign was more authentic. If we only share the great things around election time, we may not seem genuine. In fact, that tactic can smell of desperation. However, we had been sharing these great things every day for the previous two years—not because we knew it would help us in a future election—but because it was worth doing.

> **TIP**
>
> *Don't be the school that only communicates when you need something. Consistent Facebook posts throughout the year help to foster a relationship with your community.*

Facebook Likes

Beaver Local Middle School started a Facebook page in early August 2015. Until then, we had not ventured into that at a building level. But with the opening of the new K-12 facility, it seemed like the best way to get information out to people. We were running on a tight schedule to open the school, and it was critical that we get information out to the public, as well as showcase important parts of the school as everyone couldn't wait to see it. We had over 300 likes within 24 hours and currently have 540 likes in two months' time. It has served as a valuable tool to get out information as well as answer questions about a variety of items.

The power of our Facebook page has already been demonstrated several times. For example, our district participated in the See You at the Pole™ Day that is celebrated across the United States. Our postings about that event reached 20,752 people and received 406 likes with 44 positive comments. This shows the power of social media and how it reaches more people than we could have ever imagined. We also held our first all-school pep rally and posted a panoramic photo of the packed gymnasium—it was a sea of students and staff dressed in red. The post reached 5,672 people and received 138 likes. Both of these serve as examples of the power social media has to help you share your school's message.

Great things are happening in our schools. Great things are happening in *your* schools. Why would we want to keep it a secret?

See You at the Pole!

**The Benefits of Having
a Facebook Page**

**Need some help
getting started?
Watch this video tutorial**

Tips for Creating a Facebook Page

- Keep Facebook posts positive.

- Determine whether you will show faces of students in photos.

- Do not use students' first and last names.

- If you allow comments, be sure to use them as two-way communication.

- Do not engage in a Facebook argument. If necessary, pick up the phone and call the person who made a negative or concerned comment.

Chapter Six
Twitter

Tools You'll Need:
Smart phone, tablet, or computer, and Twitter app or Twitter.com

Average Time Commitment:
1 Minute per tweet

Many people unfamiliar with Twitter think it is simply a platform for celebrities to tell their fans where they are eating or who they are hanging out with. While there is no denying some people use Twitter for that purpose, it has so many more uses.

"TV beats River View 42-36."

I [Ryan] started exploring the uses of Twitter when I was the head wrestling coach at Tri-Valley High School in Dresden, Ohio, back in 2009. To be completely honest, scholastic wrestling is not the most fan-friendly sport. If you attend a basketball or football game, you are committing a few hours to attend the event. Wrestling tournaments, on the other hand, can take up an entire Saturday. That's a significant time commitment. As a result, scholastic wrestling does not usually have a huge following.

TIP

Real-time Twitter posts are great for special events and to let parents know when that field trip/game/band bus will be back at the school.

With this in mind, I began using Twitter to share updates in real-time about team and individual performances to supporters who didn't attend the tournaments. Short updates, such as "TV beats River View 42-36. The streak is over," or "Heading into the finals. TV with a 15-point lead over Marion-Franklin. TV has 8 guys alive," allowed supporters to follow the team's progress. I figured students or teachers were far more likely to check their devices for a wrestling update than they were to travel to a tournament to watch. They cared about our team and our kids; they wanted to know how our team was doing, but until we began to use social media, they usually did not learn any results until morning announcements at school the following Monday.

With posts, or *tweets*, limited to only 140 characters, Twitter forces you to keep your messages short, something users like. If you want a quick update about how a sports team is doing or some other event related to school, you get a short update and are informed. And Twitter does not limit you just to text; you can tweet photographs and short videos to your followers. Again, Twitter is more than just celebrities and their food.

Twitter and *Teach Like a PIRATE*

In 2013, I [Eric] along with the teachers and other administrators at Beaver Local started dabbling with Twitter to see if or how it could help us grow and improve. In the process, we discovered the value of an online Professional Learning Network (PLN)—a vast group of educators and leaders who support one another with ideas and information.

That network connected us with outstanding educators across Ohio and the rest of the United States. One of those educators was Dave Burgess.

That same year, we were looking for a book to guide our summer professional-development study. Since our school was moving to flexible space and learning communities, we considered a number of books on twenty-first-century learning. While on Twitter one day, I stumbled upon Dave and his book *Teach Like a PIRATE* and suggested it as our guide. The impact that book has made on both my career and my daily outlook on school has been life changing. *Teach Like a PIRATE* has also become a vital part of our school culture, as our teachers have embraced the philosophy and incorporated it into many things we do. It also convinced my fellow educators and me of the power of social media and Twitter.

As Matt Miller notes in *Ditch That Textbook*, social media opened doors I did not know existed. Miller explains that social media actually *creates* doors. That has certainly been true for me. Twitter exposed me

Twitter is a tool that empowers you to keep your stakeholders informed.

to more than I had ever learned in a class or workshop—and created doors to educators, their ideas, and best practices, thereby increasing my personal, professional development in ways I had never thought possible. Our school reached out to Dave, and he willingly joined our book studies #bltlap (Beaver Local Teach Like a PIRATE). Ryan McLane also joined us for this online study. Ryan had recently hosted the first #tlap day at his school. Having the author of the book join our chats was powerful, as was having professionals from schools across the country join in to discuss the philosophies behind *Teach Like a PIRATE.*

More conversations with Dave and Ryan followed, including Dave providing a day of professional development at our school, which Ryan also attended. My exposure to Dave and the many educators with the #tlap philosophy helped me acquire a growth mindset, something that was powerful in the classroom and in my role as an assistant principal.

It Will Spread like Wildfire!

If you are a superintendent, especially in an area where the weather can be problematic during the winter months, and you still question whether or not Twitter is an effective means of communication, try the following: in October or November, let your students, families, and teachers know you have a Twitter account. When that first two-hour delay or school closing occurs, tweet it out a few minutes before you contact the local news and radio stations—and watch what happens. That tweet will have more *favorites* and *retweets* than you ever imagined. It will spread like wildfire! Your students are checking their Twitter accounts long before they turn on the television or radio. We are not suggesting you stop using the traditional methods of communicating a school delay or closure, but this experiment demonstrates one of the many powers of Twitter.

As Ryan previously mentioned, Twitter is a great source to provide updates on sporting events for your athletic community. As the athletic director at Beaver Local, I regularly post updates from events and share schedule changes and upcoming events, so those using social media have consistent timely information.

TIP

You can decide whether or not to receive notifications on your smartphone each time someone mentions you in a tweet.

While you may not want to share your mobile number on your school website, we encourage you to provide your Twitter handle to anyone who asks. While the number of families using Twitter is not large, it seems to grow each year. This two-way communication is efficient (remember all posts are limited to 140 characters) and allows you to provide real-time information to parents and your community. Whether it's answering routine questions, such as "What time is the school musical?" or "Is the cafeteria open on the last day of school?" or posting about weather delays, Twitter is a tool that empowers you to keep your stakeholders informed.

Beaver Local Twitter

Big Walnut Intermediate Twitter

Need some help getting started? Watch this video tutorial.

Tips for Using a School Twitter Account

- Create an official district, school, or classroom Twitter account.

- Use Twitter to connect with other professionals and create your own Professional Learning Network.

- Tweet important school information and updates to staff, parents, and students.

- Keep your tweets positive.

Chapter Seven
Twitter in the Classroom

Tools You'll Need:
**Smart phone, tablet, or computer,
and Twitter app or Twitter.com**

Average Time Commitment:
1 Minute per tweet

Clearly, Twitter can be a beneficial communication tool for educators. It empowers us to quickly and efficiently connect with students and parents as well as other professional educators around the globe. But what if Twitter's potential for education went beyond simple communication? It can! We've found that Twitter can be used to engage students and enhance real-time learning opportunities.

Twitter and Super Bowl Math

This past school year, some of the Beaver Local teachers created math questions centered on Super Bowl commercials, told students there would be a chat related to the commercials, and participation was voluntary. The teachers researched the commercials ahead of time and created questions based on that information and the math concepts they were teaching. As the commercials aired during the game, students worked to connect those math concepts to the commercials. Approximately one-fourth of the students participated in the Twitter chat, working through the questions and building on one another's

Twitter can be used to engage students and enhance real-time learning opportunities.

answers in a fun, engaging lesson from the comfort of their couch on a Sunday evening.

Students found this learning experience interesting, and they wanted to join in. Parents even commented they were surprised to see their children eagerly participate in a learning activity during the big game. The students were able to demonstrate their acquired knowledge by applying it to the mathematical questions centered on the commercials, while using a favorite media platform. What a great example of a formative assessment tool wrapped in a creative *optional* homework assignment, which drew a sizable number of students to participate!

Twitter and Science and Social Studies

Teachers have also used Twitter for students to post real-world examples of what they are learning in science class. For example, students learning about erosion and weathering located photos of those things and posted them with an explanation that fit Twitter's 140-character limit. The lesson helped students apply the concepts they'd learned to the real world and express that learning in concise descriptions highlighting the scientific principles observed in the photo.

Another great interactive use of Twitter came from an instructor who used it to create real-time conversation with students during the presidential debate. Using a hashtag to make the relevant posts easy to find, this teacher's students, as well as other students in both the middle school and high school, shared what they were learning while watching the debate. Additionally, students built upon their previous knowledge through class discussions centered on the pertinent topics and issues addressed by the candidates. The instructor could then use the Twitter conversation as a springboard for class the following day, tying into what students had observed during the debate. Through this classroom discussion of what many had watched the night before, even the students without social media could have access to the conversation.

TIP

Use a hashtag (#) for your class, school, or special event to make it easy for your students and teachers to find relevant tweets.

We hope these ideas help you see that Twitter doesn't have to be about celebrities or inane chatter. On the contrary, when used intentionally, Twitter connects and engages students on a familiar platform and teaches them to concisely express their thoughts about real-world events. They consistently visit social media sites for information when they hear of breaking news. Granted, the information posted on Twitter (or any social media site for that matter) is not always completely factual, but students are able to use information, test their critical thinking skills, and collaborate with others at the same time.

Tips for Using Twitter in the Classroom

- Twitter can be used to connect current events to learning, both in and out of the classroom.

- Twitter allows students to provide real-world examples about learning to their teacher, which can be discussed in and out of the classroom.

- Twitter can be used with students to preview learning activities and serve as a "hook" to engage student interest in classroom activities.

Chapter Eight
Instagram Photos

Tools You'll Need:
**Smartphone or tablet
and Instagram app**

Average Time Commitment:
1 Minute per post

The old adage "a picture is worth a thousand words" has new meaning in the digital age. Thanks to Instagram, one of the most popular types of social media, the twenty-first century philosophy is better defined as "a picture is worth a thousand *shares.*" Pictures are a big part of what makes things go "viral" so quickly on the Internet.

If you are unfamiliar with Instagram, think of it as Twitter with pictures or fifteen-second videos. One way we use it in our schools is probably what you would expect: If we see something worth sharing, we snap a quick picture or video with our smartphones or tablets and post it on Instagram so students, parents, and our communities can see what's happening in our schools. The kids *love* it.

According to the Pew Research Center, among all adults age eighteen or older, 21 percent use Instagram[1]. While that number may not seem very large, it represents about one in five families in your school. According to that same research, nearly half of Instagram users engage with the platform daily. With that in mind, we know that if our family demographic represents the typical social media user, we are connecting with 20 percent of our students' families—10 percent of them every day. Instagram is where many of our students connect with us. They enjoy the fact they can "like" photos and see pictures and videos of what is going on in their school.

Create a "Virtual" Field Trip

Recently, I [Eric] chaperoned a student trip to Washington, D.C. and posted pictures on Instagram throughout the trip. Many of the students' parents who followed our travels via social media told me how much they enjoyed experiencing the entire trip "virtually" with their children. They also appreciated that the photos gave them access to keepsake moments. One parent kept checking back to see the updates and said it was so exciting to see the great time the students were having on their learning journey through Washington, D.C. Without the use of social media, we could not have made this experience happen in real–time for our students' families.

Throughout the trip, we posted video clips. Some were of the learning experiences we had with our tour guide. Others were of unique opportunities, such as a meeting with a Korean War veteran who shared what it was like to be a soldier in that war. Each time new photos were posted, parents and other students "liked" and commented about the images. In effect, they were experiencing the moment with us—even though we were hundreds of miles apart.

TIP

Hashtags (#) help users find related images on Instagram.

Is It Worth It?

As referenced earlier, the percentages of people using Instagram may not seem very high. It's reasonable to wonder whether it's worth using the platform to reach only 21 percent of our families.

Perhaps it wouldn't be worth the effort if using it took a considerable amount of time. In fact, both of our schools considered the time cost and had to decide if we would just be adding one more thing to our school's communication efforts. But Instagram is not time con-

From a content creation standpoint, Instagram requires very little time.

suming—unless you have an addictive personality and look at pictures all day long! From a content creation standpoint, Instagram requires very little time. A few seconds, at most, is all that is needed to take a picture, choose a photo filter effect, and add a caption. With the click of a button, I can share a photo with anyone who follows our account. When we discovered we could reach potentially one in five of our families by doing ten seconds of work, the decision was easy—yes, it is worth it!

We also know that it is likely that more parents will use Instagram in the coming years. The number of students who use Instagram has grown dramatically over the past year and continues to grow, mainly because it is picture driven and is a quick, easy way to share information.

"Perfect Day"

At Big Walnut Intermediate, we have a school Instagram account, and several teachers have classroom accounts. Some teachers have individual classroom accounts, while other teachers share an account with their teaching team, so they all have access to post and share news and images from their classes.

You will have to determine how much information you want to include in the captions. Our captions are simply general descriptions of photos. We also post captions that tie pictures to quotes about character traits, reinforcing positive messages and encouraging students to be the best they can be. Some schools do not associate any names with the photographs. Some schools only use a student's first name. Each district must decide what's best for its student community.

Change the Trend

We believe it's critical to take every advantage to expose the celebrations happening in our schools and highlight our amazing young people and staff. Our lives are consumed by negative messages from the news media, gossip, and even social media. Instagram gives us one more opportunity to change that trend and share what is good and right. Along with other social media, it allows us to shift negative discussions to positive conversations (or to *start* conversations) about our schools. At a time when you would be lucky if the local newspaper covered your school a handful of times in a school year, Instagram offers daily and unlimited coverage of current information and highlights of your school to an audience of all your stakeholders.

**Beaver Local
on Instagram**

**Big Walnut Intermediate
on Instagram**

**Need some help
getting started? Check
out this tutorial.**

Tips for Using Instagram

- Determine if you are going to identify students in the captions.

- Captions don't have to be long. Users are often most engaged by short, simple descriptions.

- Have some fun and use the photo filters to enhance your photos.

Chapter Nine

Instagram Daily Message

Tools You'll Need:
Smartphone or tablet
and Instagram app

Average Time Commitment:
3 Minutes per post

We believe it is important to spread positive messages to combat the negative ones that people so often make their focus. Getting daily positive messages to students at school, however, can be difficult. So we decided to go where the students are: Instagram. To promote a positive culture in our schools, we post daily messages that focus on character and optimism. Instagram allows us to customize a message and efficiently reach a large number of young people. We've found it most effective to time these messages so that our students see them when they are a "captive" audience, such as when they're on the bus to or from school.

Wake Up—Check the Smartphone

If you have ever been around teenagers, you know one of the first things they do when they wake up in the morning is check their

One of the first things students do when they wake up in the morning is check their phones.

phones. The second thing they do—ten seconds later—is swipe the screen to refresh it and check again. This is the untapped potential of Instagram—an opportunity for us as a school, district, or classroom teacher to use it to start our students' day on a positive note.

We also use images and messages to inspire students. We post character messages or motivational quotes, so when students see images representing the district, they also see positive messages that we hope will reinforce character building.

In addition to simply snapping a photo, you can create images to post on your Instagram account in a variety of ways. Keynote is a slideshow app that makes it easy to create a simple quote. Once you have created the slide, you can take a screenshot on your device, which saves it as an image in your camera roll. You can then access the photo from Instagram. Other programs, like Canva (Canva.com), allow you to create quote images that are more visually appealing. Canva includes ready-made templates, so you just change the text to say what you want.

Positive Daily Message on Instagram

I [Ryan] admit I was skeptical about using Instagram in this manner at first. I believed students would much rather see photographs of their friends than a graphic of a positive message. But I was wrong. Instagram's instant feedback, based on the number of "likes" a photograph receives, revealed (to my surprise) that our followers "liked" the positive messages far more than the photographs of students we posted. Do not get me wrong; the photographs were popular, but the positive messages were even *more* popular! And even though the number of likes is impressive, the best part is knowing that our students are seeing these positive, empowering messages regularly.

If the students were not "liking" the daily messages, we may have worried they made a negative impression of their school and its use of Instagram. However, we saw the opposite. Our belief is that if we legitimately help only one or two students have a better day, the few minutes required to create a daily message are absolutely worth our time.

I [Eric] discovered the power of this positive message through an unforeseen circumstance at our school this year. Due to issues created from a leak in our building, students were moved to our high school, requiring a change in our regular daily school schedule—for about two weeks. To ensure teachers still got their allotted planning time, I provided instruction to students each day, using Instagram as a platform for my character-based lessons on optimism, leaders and followers, and taking a positive approach to living. Students consumed those messages in large numbers and even posted their own character messages related to the lessons. Again, our kids were

Instagram in the Classroom

buying in—in part because we were using *their* tools. Students created positive message boards with nuggets they took away from the class or a favorite quote they found on the Internet. I took pictures of these character boards daily and posted them for everyone to see.

On what was to be my final day in the classroom, students approached me to present a petition they had signed which requested that the "class" continue. Students got excited about this blend of social media, mainly through Instagram, with their classroom learning—something we hope to build upon in the future.

Oh, No—Not the Principal's Office!

Another way we use Instagram to promote positives over negatives is to combat the stereotypical image of principals being the "mean, scary person" students go see when they are in trouble. We take pride in *not* fitting that stereotype—and even correct people when they infer it, so they can avoid reinforcing a negative image. We want youngsters to know that even though we are the people who sometimes have to work with students when they need to make improved choices, we deeply care about them. We want to be seen as positive figures. To that end, our goal is to interact with every student daily, though our other responsibilities often make that difficult. Instagram gives us one more avenue to ensure we connect with them on a daily basis. In fact, we continue to send positive messages throughout the summer months, so students see that we are invested in them.

"Show Power of Social Media!"

Almost all of our schools' Instagram followers are district students and parents—exactly the audience we want to see and hear our messages about learning *and* fun and the positive character traits we want to foster. A recent event confirmed that our key stakeholders are getting our message on a daily basis via Instagram: While at a conference, we presented a session about the impact of social media. As we spoke, a staff member posted an Instagram picture of Eric speaking. The caption encouraged our followers to "...show power of social media. Hurry!" In ten minutes, the photo had 175 likes, and, likely, countless others had viewed the photo. That's powerful!

We've discovered students are eager to be their best. Sometimes, as educators, we need to connect their passions with experiences to enable them to see that the work needed to reach their potential is well worth the effort. At our schools, that connection comes through classroom activities and by relating those activities to their world. Social media tools—Instagram being a key platform—empower us to do that. Students certainly have the potential to misuse these tools, but students have also misused pencils and paper throughout history. Our duty is to teach them the proper uses of social media. Modeling this while we engage with students, enables us to expand the power of social media through education, rather than restricting it by removing students' power to connect.

Tips for Using Instagram

- Instagram can be used to convey a positive message daily to your school community.

- Instagram can be used to highlight positive messages and events *within* your school.

- Instagram allows educators to stay connected to students year round.

- Instagram provides a platform to reinforce the culture of character you want to build in your school community.

Chapter Ten

Instagram Photo Feedback

Tools You'll Need:
**Smartphone or tablet
and Instagram app**

Average Time Commitment:
1 Minute per post

Some of life's greatest discoveries often happen by accident. We are not claiming that using Instagram to get feedback is one of the world's greatest discoveries, but it has been very useful to us, and we discovered this application completely by accident.

From Furniture to Flipboard to Feedback Frenzy

Beaver Local was in the design phase of a new K-12 school—a building intended to look very different from that of traditional schools. A key part of this design was the creation of learning communities with flexible space. The architects had asked me [Eric] to build a Flipboard magazine with video and images of furniture for the new facility. (See Chapter 13 for more about Flipboard.) The easiest way to do this was to post pictures to Instagram and then post them to the magazine. As I posted these pictures to Instagram, students immediately liked and commented on the pictures, sharing their input on the photos of classroom furniture. I then posted a picture with a caption *asking* students to "Please comment," which generated even more comments from students and staff. Suddenly, I thought, "Maybe we are onto something."

TIP

Asking people to click, share, or comment significantly increases engagement. Don't be shy. Tell people what you want them to do.

By posting photos on Instagram, we were able to use Flipboard to create a digital magazine, which was then used by the architects to showcase furniture to our staff as they chose pieces for the new building. Much of the furniture was flexible in nature and served multiple purposes, a fact that created a lot of buzz among staff and students. Using Instagram gave students the opportunity to have input, which, in turn, generated excitement about the new facility. The architects also gave our staff the ability to flip through Flipboard and see interactive videos along with the images, so they could see the functionality of the furniture to be used at the new facility. Staff members saw the furniture choices in the interactive magazine, and they were able to view the number of students who had liked the photos and read the comments that students had posted on Instagram.

Another benefit of this interactive feedback process was the ability to see quick, fifteen-second videos that showed how the furniture worked in a variety of settings. Because of social media, our staff, students, and the architects collaborated on a very important project; all of our stakeholders were able to provide input. At the same time, the experience reaffirmed to everyone involved how powerful and beneficial social media tools can be when used properly.

What's for Lunch?

We used Instagram for feedback again recently when our school was looking to bring a nutrition service group into the district to assist with our school lunch program. The group came to a school board meeting to share their proposal, present what they had to offer, and provide samples for those in attendance. Students and parents were willing participants and offered positive feedback about the samples. While we snacked, I took a picture and posted it to Instagram.

Check out what's for lunch!

Almost instantly, it had thirty-three likes from students who were not at the board meeting. Soon, the conversation spilled into other social media sites, as well. What began with students and parents sharing on social media about what they were seeing and tasting at the meeting, led to positive discussions about the options—most notably that the food samples appeared more appealing than some of the traditional school lunch options. Even though this board meeting took place during the middle of the summer, the use of Instagram

Social media offers multiple benefits for education when we connect passion and purpose for our stakeholders.

and Facebook generated conversation and attention from parents and students about an important item for the upcoming school year. Even those who weren't in attendance were able to weigh in and help us promote the upcoming changes in a positive manner.

This type of conversation and feedback from parents and students is a good way to gather information for decisions and promote your school programs. Social media offers multiple benefits for education when we connect passion and purpose for our stakeholders. It allows us to create a common foundation for students and staff to build upon. The ability to reach so many people in a quick and efficient manner allows users to generate feedback and connection and create interest and excitement about any school program or event.

Tips for Using Instagram for Feedback

- Instagram (and other social media platforms) allows users to gather feedback from all stakeholders at their convenience.

- Feedback, in the format of comments and likes, can be used for decision making.

- Social media serves as a tool for public relations.

- Images and short videos can provide information to assist in decisions.

- Information can be shared quickly and efficiently.

Chapter Eleven
Instagram in the Classroom

Tools You'll Need:
**Smartphone or tablet
and Instagram app**

Average Time Commitment:
3-5 Minutes per post

So far we've talked about how Instagram can be used to inspire and inform students and their families. The platform is also a flexible tool that can be used for educational purposes. For example, some teachers use Instagram to post images that serve as *hooks* for lessons and promote learning in the classroom. Others use it to allow students to preview upcoming material. Some teachers use Flipagram, which compiles videos and photos in a quick slideshow format, complete with music to feature projects from the beginning to the end and spotlight student work in an engaging manner. Teachers also post real-life examples of topics discussed in the classroom— from weather and erosion to economics.

**Instagram in the
Classroom**

Some teachers post questions on both Twitter and Instagram to engage students during non-school hours, while others use Instagram to post annotations from classwork so students have access to homework when absent or for extra assistance.

Nothing but Net...or Backboard Buster?

One example that connected the many uses of Instagram in the classroom came in the form of a math hook. A teacher created a video of a student shooting a basketball but stopped the video before the ball reached the hoop. The following day, the teacher began her class with the video and added the mathematical formula needed to determine if the shot was nothing but net

Will it Hit the Hoop?

or a backboard buster. She then posted this using Explain Everything, so the annotations were seen on the photo and video.

The possibilities for using these tools to engage students and pique their interest are limitless. Instagram (and social media in general) is an ever developing platform used by teachers to demonstrate learning opportunities for students.

Instagram is a tool used by some instructors at BLMS to highlight positive learning in the classroom. Students see their instructors highlighting the great work they are doing in the classroom. Teachers also use this popular platform to enhance rapport with students by connecting with them in a format they already like and use.

Additionally, educators can use Instagram to throw out a hook the night before to excite students about upcoming learning opportunities. We have personally seen many examples of kids rushing to class because the teacher posted a photo tease on Instagram the night before.

**Create Hooks
with Instagram**

Tips for Using Instagram in the Classroom

- Post photos to create energy around activities that increase student interest for the next day's class.

- Post photos to connect to real-world authentic learning.

- Post photos that feature student projects to highlight their efforts.

Chapter Twelve
Hashtags (#)

Tools You'll Need:
Facebook, Twitter, Instagram, and many other social media platforms use hashtags.

Average Time Commitment:
<1 Minute

Pop quiz: Do you know your school's or district's mission? Could you recite it if you had to?

#missionmatters

I [Ryan] spent eight years teaching in a school district where I could not have told you one word of its mission statement. I then moved on to another district where I spent four years. Again, I could not have given you a single word from that district's mission statement. Even as a junior-high principal for two years, I have no recollection of that school district's mission statement. How refreshing to spend only two hours in the Big Walnut Local School District and be able to recite—along with everyone else associated with the district—its mission statement: *inspire and guide*.

Do you know *and believe in* your organization's mission statement? Or is it just words on a piece of paper? Mission statements often sound like a mouthful of words created years ago which, for whatever reason, we do not feel the need to update or make more user friendly. That's sad! One of the most important elements of a positive organizational culture is creating a shared vision and a mission that stakeholders can recite and believe in.

When I came to Big Walnut, the words *inspire and guide* were everywhere—on the letterhead, in every e-mail, staff update, and signage. The mission statement can be seen in practically every building. More importantly, everyone buys into the shared vision of the school district. Ask any secretary, custodian, teacher, administrator—or even student—what the Big Walnut mission is, and they will likely respond with "inspire and guide."

Beaver Local Middle School's theme for the 2014-2015 school year was "you matter." To be fair, each student had always mattered, but that had never been verbalized. In the 2014-2015 school year, this theme became very apparent because of how it was messaged by the administrative team at the school. One of the most effective ways they made sure students got the message was through the use of a hashtag (#).

Hashtags can be a great way to promote a central idea to your students and also serve to organize social media posts for your school community. Hashtags provide users with a way to make sure their pictures are included with the school platform. Staff, students—anyone—can search for or click on your school's hashtag and find every message associated with that hashtag.

Hashtags provide users with a way to make sure their pictures are included with the school platform.

#blmsyoumatter #inspireandguide

At Beaver Local Middle School, we began using the hashtag: *#blmsyoumatter*. My staff and I [Eric] chose this hashtag because we wanted one that served as a central theme to everything we do with students and was something we could build upon. We strive to make sure students know they each matter and can make a difference. Their impact is measured by what they accomplish, regardless of what others do. We want students to see they control their actions, and on a daily basis, they can make a positive impact.

This hashtag is attached to all images and tweets we post representing our school and students, as well as the character messages posted on all of our social media platforms. Over time, the hashtag has evolved into something we include in e-mails and in written notes. We want to constantly reinforce the message that everyone matters and connect this belief to the message that no kind gesture or word is too small to make an impact.

TIP

Use your hashtag on ALL relevant social media posts to make it easy for people to find and recognize your message.

We also use a specific hashtag for tweets and Instagram messages for field trips. During the field trip to Washington, D.C., the hashtag allowed students and parents to view all the messages from the trip by either clicking on the hashtag or simply typing it into a search on Twitter or Instagram. Parents and students could see all the images and messages from the trip, regardless of who they followed or what messages were posted. The posts could then be turned into a Flipboard magazine, which gave all students, parents, and staff a complete digital memento of their experience.

Hashtags promote a sense of community within our schools. Because they make it easy to find images or quotes shared by students and staff, hashtags also promote collaboration. With a quick search, I can find posts worth retweeting, "liking," or adding into our school Flipboard magazine. These platforms become a school-wide resource available to and created by all staff and students. And because the community helps create this pool of information, images, and inspiration, each member feels a sense of ownership. Once again, these efforts to share and communicate reinforce with students the positive power of social media and how these tools can be used to connect to make an impact.

Another example of a district-wide hashtag is Big Walnut's use of *#inspireandguide*. When anyone in this school district sees something exemplifying what the district stands for, they can add the hashtag *#inspireandguide* and share it, regardless of the type of social media platform.

#wehaditfirst

Before using a hashtag or creating your own, be sure to see if anyone else is already using it. No one necessarily owns the rights to a hashtag, but you want to avoid confusion. For example, when we were initially creating a hashtag at Big Walnut, we thought *#wearebw* would be great. Initially it was—until I [Ryan] noticed tweets with the same hashtag coming from college students at Baldwin Wallace University. I wasn't about to tell some college students, "we had it first!" So we chose a hashtag that no one else was using.

In short, a hashtag can be a way to brand your school or district. The hashtag allows students to know they can share any picture or great message with everyone in your district on social media by simply adding that hashtag to their post. It also allows you to catalog social media messages, making it easier to import into Flipboard, should you choose to create your own digital magazine.

Tips for Using a Hashtag

- Create a unique hashtag that will be associated with your district, school, or classroom.

- Promote the hashtag so that others within your community can use it.

Chapter Thirteen

Flipboard

Tools You'll Need:
Smartphone or tablet and Flipboard app

Average Time Commitment:
10 Minutes

Flipboard, an online magazine which flips like turning pages of a magazine, is a great tool that allows you to customize what you see by interest level, so you can regularly read about subjects you enjoy. You can also explore magazines custom-built by others about a variety of subjects which may interest you. The platform allows you to link to and share from your other social media accounts, including Facebook, Instagram, and Twitter. Plus, it offers the opportunity to save pictures you have liked, favorited, tweeted, or posted and either add to your camera roll or build them into magazines. These magazines become an interactive, easy-to-update yearbook, highlighting pictures and videos from your school year.

Members can follow for free and receive updates of current articles as well as the most recent tweets, messages, photos, and videos. Your followers can see daily events and also have a year-end keepsake. Other Flipboard users can access your digital magazine and "flip" through the pages you have created. Even people who don't have the Flipboard app can see your compiled images online when you share a link with them.

Flipboard for Field Trips

Flipboard, along with Instagram and Twitter, is another great tool to create interactive field trips. Beaver Local Middle School has used these tools during the past couple of years to enhance students' educational experiences during the annual eighth-grade trip to Washington, D.C. Last year was the first year I [Eric] attended the trip, and I wanted to create an uncommon experience for our students—I wanted to make our trip something everyone would remember. One way I did that was to use Twitter and Instagram to create an interactive journey through the many landmarks we would visit. This adventure included facts, questions, pictures, and selfies!

We posted pictures on Twitter and Instagram and added quotes which represented Jefferson, King, Roosevelt, and Lincoln. We also asked questions such as, "Why did the sculptor of Lincoln's statue choose to make Lincoln strong on the one side and relaxed on the other?" and "Do you believe these former leaders would be successful today? Why or why not?" Students were encouraged to share their insights, based on what they learned on the trip and at school, as well as their own opinions. These activities encouraged students to discuss the topics with one another and to explore the Internet to find facts to support their thoughts and opinions.

Another benefit of using social media on this trip was that it allowed our group to interact with our eighth-grade social studies teacher who also happened to be in Washington, D.C. He had attended this same eighth-grade trip a few years ago with students who were now in high school, and because of their rapport, he had been invited to accompany them on their high school trip to D.C. Using the hashtag we created, he posted images, facts, questions, and comments through-out the trip related to what our middle school students were experi-

D.C. Trip Flipboard

encing. His posts also exposed them to some of the differences between the two trips. For instance, the high school's visit to Mount Vernon related to much of what the eighth graders had learned about President Washington throughout the school year. Students were excited to interact with their teacher as well as with the other students on our trip.

The Principal's Taking a Selfie?

I used to say I would never take a selfie. There was also a time when I believed I would never text—or use social media in schools. But just like my embracing social media and texting, during this trip I decided to flip the camera and try to create an illusion of exhibits being closer to us than they actually were. I never could have guessed how excited the students would get over me snapping a selfie! Once again, I was

> **Students excitedly posed for selfies with their teachers and principal, an experience that allowed us to connect with them on their terms and build rapport.**

entering their world and connecting with them in a way that surprised and delighted them. Students excitedly posed for selfies with their teachers and principal, an experience that allowed us to connect with them on their terms and build rapport. In *Teach Like a PIRATE*, Dave Burgess mentions that each minute spent informally with a student is worth ten hours of class time. These selfies were no different. A quick moment taken to snap and alter the picture completely changed the students' outlook on what we were doing. At the same time, we showed how the pictures depicted learning and character building, ensuring that students made the connection between learning *and* fun.

Beaver QR Code

We added another twist this year to create excitement about the trip and the keepsake Flipboard magazine. Our local T-shirt store knew our magazine from the previous year was well received, and they suggested incorporating a QR code. We created a QR code using our mascot, the Beaver, which students could scan and be taken directly to the magazine. This year, the students wore color-coded shirts each day with the QR code located at the bottom of the shirt. Students could scan their friends' shirts or their own to see the entire trip without even having to type in a web address. As an added benefit, the QR scanning modeled another way we can use technology to enhance what we do.

D.C. Field Trip T-Shirt with QR Code

Flipboard Memory Book

At Beaver Local Middle School, using our hashtag with Twitter and Instagram has led to creating a daily magazine highlighting the entire year, in pictures and in short videos, with positive messages mixed throughout. The magazine is especially popular among parents because it is free and includes events from the beginning to the end of the school year. The flipping feature makes it interactive, and it offers the school community an up–to-date account of the school year at any point in the year.

TIP

Make it easy for your community members to find you. Set up all your social media accounts with the same name and use the same school hashtag.

Because Twitter and Instagram are linked to Flipboard, only a few brief moments are needed to keep the magazine up-to-date on a daily basis. The cover can be customized, and readers have the ability to look back through their favorite moments from the school year.

Need help getting started? Check out this video tutorial.

Tips for Making a Flipboard Digital Magazine

- Share the link to your Flipboard magazine so that non-Flipboard users can access the content.

- Photos will not automatically appear in Flipboard. You will choose the photos you want to add to your Flipboard magazine.

- If multiple people are using a common hashtag, you will be able to choose any of those photos to add to your magazine.

Chapter Fourteen
The School Blog

Tools You'll Need:
Computer or tablet and blogging platform

Average Time Commitment:
30 minutes

A s you can likely tell, one of the recurring themes of this book is the importance of sharing the great things happening in today's schools. A blog is another vehicle to use for this purpose. As educators who are constantly trying to learn new things, we really enjoy reading other educators' blogs. Sometimes a blog is used to give an opinion on educational policy; however, some of my favorite blogs are those by fellow educators who share best practices.

In my [Ryan] fourth year as a principal, I decided to try to use a school blog to tell our school's story in more detail than I could through simply a photograph or a video. Starting with the blog's title—*180 Days Of Awesome*—we were sending a message that great things were happening in our school every day, and we were going to use this blog to share those great things.

TIP

Blog posts don't have to be long. Limit blog posts to 300-500 words. Even a single photo with a caption will work!

The Lone Duck

One such "great thing" was the story related to a photo I took during recess on the day of the 2015 College Football National Championship—the day Ohio State was playing the Oregon Ducks. As we have mentioned previously, there is power in social media, and the exposure this photo received is an excellent example. One of our students was a huge Oregon fan. With our school located about twenty minutes north of the Ohio State University campus, well, he was the *only* student wearing an Oregon jersey that day.

When I told our Oregon fan about a staged school picture I had seen in which one student in an Ohio elementary class wearing a Michigan shirt (Ohio State's chief rival) was isolated off to the side in the class photo, he thought it would be hilarious to recreate it—this time with Ohio State fans and the lone Oregon fan. We looked for students who were wearing Ohio State jerseys (it wasn't difficult to find quite a few!) and gathered them in the gym during lunch to snap the photo.

A few hours after I tweeted the photo, we were on ESPN's *SportsCenter*.

Our school blog was the perfect platform to share how the interesting events unfolded. For example, the picture snapped during lunch went viral and opened the door for me to speak to a radio station in Portland, Oregon, about how our kids love to come to school because they learn *and*

BWI Makes ESPN

have fun. I was able to share that same message with the producers at ESPN when they contacted me for permission to use the photo. I also used our school blog to explain the *why* behind the photo. No, I was not promoting or condoning bullying in our school. Of course, no one from our school or community expressed those concerns. Because we share school happenings with them nearly every day, they are fully aware of the positive school culture we have created.

Students Tell Their Stories

The school blog is a way for principals to tell their school's story and for students, families, and others to share *their* take on what is happening at their school. To make sure students at my school are empowered to share their perspective, I routinely ask them to write blog posts. I will never forget the first time I asked a student to do this. The student was a fifth grader, so Big Walnut Intermediate was new to him and his 280 classmates. When I asked him on a Friday afternoon if he would be interested in writing a school blog post, he seemed happy to oblige. Since our school is a Google Apps For Education (GAFE) school, I told him simply to write his post in a Google Doc and share it with me when he finished. I also sent his parents an e-mail letting them know I asked him to do this, giving them more information. After that, I did not give it a second thought.

The next day, two e-mails stood out in my inbox. One was an e-mail notification that this student had shared a document with me. The second was from the student's mother.

In her e-mail, she thanked me for giving her son the opportunity to write a post for the school blog but went on to share something even more powerful. Her son had always loved coming to school, but she had never seen him as excited as he had been during his first week at Big Walnut. She told me that as soon as he came home from school on Friday, he went to work on his blog post, spending more time on a Friday doing "school work" than she could ever remember. He then woke up early the next morning to revise his post and even enlisted the assistance of his father to help him proofread his piece.

This is powerful to me because, first of all, this kid was a good kid, so he was not writing the post so that I would "owe" him in the future. Secondly, I was his principal, not his teacher, so agreeing to do this— and doing it with such thoughtfulness and effort—was not going to impact his grade. He wanted to do it because it was something unique. He was given a platform to tell *his* story and was very excited to do so. How did I know he was genuinely excited? My first clue was his spending a few hours on a weekend to create something that wasn't for a grade. Additionally, it was a family bonding experience. He spent time, actually multiple times, over the weekend talking to his family about the positive things he was seeing and experiencing in school.

I wish I could tell you the school blog was another completely successful social media platform we implemented in our school, but I would be lying. I made a major mistake in the first year of implementing the school blog: I did not give up enough control. As a result, the blog stopped happening—not because it was a poor idea but because of poor execution and planning on my part. During the 2014-2015 school year, state testing changed formats and became computerized and took an enormous amount of my time. As a result, I put the school blog on the back burner—an avoidable mistake. Compared to social media posts, the school blog took a lot of time to create. I stopped writing blog posts for one of the same reasons I gave up paper and e-mail newsletters—it was time consuming.

TIP

You don't have to be the one to write every post. Invite students, other teachers, even parents to be guest bloggers on your site.

And I learned a valuable lesson from the experience: I needed to give up some control. The blog needed less posts from me and more posts from our students and even teachers and other staff members. They have stories to tell, and the vast majority are eager and willing to share. Many of them are just waiting to be asked. This coming school year, I will be asking—a lot.

The Senior Experience

The Madison Local School District, a small rural district in southwestern Ohio, morphed the idea of a student-run blog into an experience—*The Senior Experience* to be exact. Created by AJ Huff, the district's Coordinator of School-Community Relations, *The Senior Experience* has become a course through which students tell their school's story and use many of the twenty-first-century tools and skills described in this book to do so.

The Senior Experience gives six diverse seniors access to the district's website to blog about their senior school year. They write about the great things happening to them personally and about the positive happenings at Madison High School. They are sharing these experiences with their friends, family members, community, and anyone else who cares to read their stories.

Madison Local School District is unique in that it resides in an area that does not have a traditional town. A few gas stations and a small food mart exist, but most residents drive across the river to the small city of Middletown to do their shopping and dining. As such, the opportunity for residents to meet at the local restaurant, barber shop, or pub does not really exist, so the opportunity for conversations about the schools does not happen in those venues either.

Many residents of Madison who have ties to the schools do gather at youth and school-sponsored athletic events, but those who do not have a connection to the schools do not always attend those events.

One could argue there is a disconnect between a large contingent of the community and the school district. How can a school in this type of environment reach the disconnected portion of the community? AJ Huff is using social media and *The Senior Experience* to help bridge that gap. While the residents of Madison may not have a "downtown" to gather in and share stories, they do have the Internet.

Many educators, especially at the high school level, are hesitant about implementing the use of social media because of the potentially negative "what ifs?" Again, we encourage you also to consider all of the potentially *positive* "what ifs?" before discounting its use. Madison and *The Senior Experience* are just one of many examples of the successful implementation of social media in a high school setting.

Tips for Creating a School or Class Blog

- Choose the blogging platform (Wordpress, Blogger) that best suits your needs.

- When opportunity arises, give students owner-ship to assist in using social media and having them model the benefits.

- Use the blog as a way to share more of the story than was originally shared in a photo or video.

Chapter Fifteen
Periscope

Tools You'll Need:
**Smartphone or tablet
and Periscope app**

Average Time Commitment:
1 Minute

Have you ever been somewhere and wished you could visually share your experience in real time? We are not talking about recording a video and uploading it to YouTube or Facebook for people to view after the fact. We are talking about *live*.

Periscope is an app you can link with your Twitter account to give you the ability to broadcast things live with very little setup. Justin Buttermore, the Athletic Director and head football coach at Tri-Valley High School in Dresden, Ohio, learned about Periscope when it came out in the spring of 2015 and began experimenting with it. One of his first uses of Periscope demonstrates its power and usefulness.

Capturing History in the Making

Tri-Valley had a senior discus thrower attempting to be the first female state champion in school history. She was a two-time, state runner-up, and the defending state champion was back to defend her title. If the Tri-Valley athlete achieved something no other female athlete in school history had done, she was going to have to beat the best.

In past years, the outcome of the event would have spread like wildfire through texts and social media, like Twitter and Instagram, and a recorded video would have probably popped up as well. But the downside of that scenario is the event is over. And the best part of an athletic event like this is the anticipation and excitement in the moment it is happening. Tri-Valley decided to use Periscope to make this real-life, real-time moment available to more people.

With each throw of the discus, classmates, staff members, and people in the community watched the athlete live as she tried to make school history. And history is exactly what they saw as this young lady pulled off the upset and won her first state title! Periscope allowed virtually anyone interested to share this exciting moment because someone at the event used his mobile phone to broadcast it live.

Who's Broadcasting?

Newness is one issue that could complicate using Periscope. Many state and school organizations do not know what to make of it yet. Periscope is on their radars, but they have very few formal policies in place to restrict its use. When we contacted a member of the Ohio High School Athletic Association (OHSAA) to ask whether or not a school's use of Periscope would violate any broadcasting rights, they did not think it would be a violation because it would be too difficult for them to monitor.

Note: If a major high school athletic event is being televised, using Periscope could be a violation of broadcast rights. If other means of broadcast for an event exist, skip Periscope. Avoid competing with major television stations; if the event is being televised, your key stakeholders have a way to watch it. Using Periscope to broadcast the discus throw at the state finals was a legitimate use of this tool because the broadcasting rights had not been sold to a television station and, other

---

You can use Periscope to offer students experiences and exposure to ideas, events, and places they would not otherwise have.

---

than attending the event in person, no other means were available to watch the event. It is in your best interest to check with your state's official, athletic, sanctioning body before broadcasting any event on Periscope. And if no restrictions prevent you from broadcasting the event, it's in your community's best interest to take advantage of this powerful tool.

Special Considerations

If you use Periscope, you have a few options to consider before beginning your broadcast. Do you want to share your location? Do you want your broadcast to be viewed by anyone or only those you follow and you select? Do you want to allow comments from anyone or only those you follow? Do you want Twitter to automatically tweet a link of your broadcast? Periscope allows you to customize these options as you prefer. Additionally, your broadcast will be available to viewers on Periscope for twenty-four hours; however, you can also save your broadcast to your device's camera roll and share it through other means, such as uploading it to your school's website or Facebook page.

Another consideration when using Periscope is to make sure you are not broadcasting a student who is on the "no image use" list. The last thing you want to do is Periscope a class and have a student on the "no image use" list walk by the camera.

Not Just for PR

At Big Walnut Intermediate School, we have used Periscope to broadcast teaching practices I [Ryan] felt were worth sharing. My intent was not public relations but rather to share some of our teachers' practices with other interested educators. Because we do a good job promoting the great things our teachers are doing via social media, educators from around the state visit our school frequently to see the innovative practices being implemented in our classrooms.

Joe Mazza recently organized the #EdCampLdr camps across the United States. During these conferences, many great minds in education shared their ideas and innovative practices. Event coordinators used social media, including Twitter and Periscope, to broadcast live from the conferences, so viewers could attend the sessions and learn from the presenters virtually. This real-time platform gives educators the ability to learn directly from the experts and attend events they may have otherwise missed.

Imagine how you can use Periscope to offer students experiences and exposure to ideas, events, and places they would not otherwise have because of financial or travel limitations. Periscope and other video services (e.g., Skype and Google Hangout) open doors for students to connect with others in ways not previously available to them.

**Need help getting
started? Check out this
video tutorial.**

Tips for Using Periscope

- Be sure no one has the rights to what you are broadcasting on Periscope.

- Determine if you will allow comments to be broadcast.

- In advance, promote an event you will be broadcasting on Periscope.

- The broadcast will remain on Periscope for a short period of time (twenty-four hours as of the printing of this book).

Chapter Sixteen
Bringing It All Together

Technology is terrific; it's another superpower for our teacher superhero toolbox! However, the educator is the most important part of this equation. We must model the use of technology and find ways to show students how they can use it effectively to interact collaboratively and grow and enhance their learning beyond what they dreamed possible. We educators often say students know more about technology than we do. While this is often true, they still need us to guide them in using technology to discover ideas and practices that can make them better professionals and people and, ultimately, to become lifelong learners.

As we said at the beginning of the book, using social media is not an all-or-nothing proposition. Honestly, if you are not currently using social media and you try to implement everything we discussed at once, you likely will be unsuccessful. The key is to determine which one or two methods are the best fit for your particular situation and start from there. Start small, using a platform you are familiar with, and build upon what you feel enhances the impact you want to make on students, staff, parents, and community members. As you grow more comfortable, move on to other platforms and continue to educate yourself about different social media outlets. Evaluate, through discussions and observation, the reactions of your students and families so you can continue to connect and make a positive impact.

If you *are* using social media already, can you expand your use of current tools? For example, could you initiate a daily positive message with Instagram? We were already using Instagram, but I [Ryan] had not thought to use the daily positive message. Eric was posting a daily positive message and appeared to be having success with it in his school. Choosing to post a daily message, for me, didn't require learning a new tool; I was simply using an existing tool in a different manner. If you are starting from scratch, have no fear! We were all beginners at one time. The first thing you need to decide is with whom you want to share your stories. With your audience in mind, you can begin choosing the tools that will make the biggest impact.

Once you become comfortable with a variety of social media platforms, you will be amazed by your story's reach. Some of our families watch our video newsletter because we post it on Facebook. Others see it when we tweet out the link, while others see it because they subscribe to our YouTube Channel. Few of our families use all three of those, but because we are using a variety of tools, we are reaching them where they are.

The Senior Experience at Madison High School is a perfect example of a school using a variety of social media platforms and tying them all together with a hashtag. Madison chose #goodtobeamohawk, Mohawk being their school's mascot. Their students have an opportunity to tell their school's story through a blog, Facebook, Twitter, and Instagram. By using a variety of tools, they are communicating with a large group of their stakeholders.

**Check out
The Senior Experience.**

Evolving—but Here to Stay

Social media is always evolving—a truth that is important to remember as you begin exploring the options discussed in this book. Five years ago, Facebook would have been the best option for sharing stories with your students. However, it would not have been the best place to share with parents and grandparents. Today, that has changed. In fact, seniors are the fastest growing demographic on social media today[1] and Facebook is their prime location. We regularly talk to our students—the group we believe to be the most knowledgeable about social media—and ask them to educate us about new platforms that we're unfamiliar with. We also ask students for their ideas about how these platforms could be used in school. Not every platform serves the purpose of connecting and building rapport with students and our stakeholders, but it is important to be willing to dive into this social media world and see what does work. Diving in may require us to take risks and open our communities to real-world, real-time connection. You may find, as we did with the traditional, paper and e-mail newslet-

Platforms will change, but social media is here to stay.

ters, that the impact of a particular medium is not significant enough to make it worth doing. And that is okay. Try something different until you find what works for you. Platforms will change, but social media is here to stay. People crave it and are going to use it. As educators and leaders in our communities, we have an opportunity to create a positive culture of social media use.

Remember also that while these platforms and tools will constantly change, people's desire for information and a positive culture will remain the same. Dave Burgess states in *Teach Like a PIRATE*, "Don't hang around negative people; they will sap your super powers as sure as kryptonite."[2] Social media is our new super power and can help us maintain a positive culture. We feel strongly that the time invested in these tools is well worth the return. Making daily connections through social media with large numbers of community members helps us turn negative positions into positive ones. Just as there is power in a positive phone call or short written note, we are finding the power in positive messages sent through social media. The difference is that social media allows that message to be shared countless times. Students see you investing in them. They see you connecting with them in ways they do not expect from school. This connection is unique and creates a sense of community that would not exist without social media tools.

We know that our school story will be told, and our school story matters. We want to make sure we are the authors of that story and our staff and students are the main characters. Everyone has a best seller in their community. We want to make sure our best seller is available for everyone to read!

Tips for Bringing It All Together

- A common hashtag among platforms is a great way to bring various platforms of social media together.

- Keep the messages positive.

- Get students involved as much as possible and as much as is permissible.

- Educate families about the different social media platforms, but do not force them to go to any one in particular. You need to go where they are.

- Start slow and expand from there.

Chapter Seventeen
Call to Action

In spite of knowing the expression about what happens when a person assumes, as we wrote this book, we felt pretty confident making one assumption: we assume you have great stories about your schools to share with your community. You want to tell those stories. You *need* to tell those stories. However, if you have difficulty identifying stories worth sharing, you need to start there. As the old expression states: "Not even the best chef in the world can make chicken salad out of chicken 'feathers.'" Social media is a good tool, but it is not *that* good—it cannot make stories from nothing. Our guess is, though, when you start reflecting on your classrooms, school programs, students, teachers, and districts, you will find some amazing stories to share!

Getting Started

The first step toward sharing your stories via social media is to begin having conversations with the decision makers in your district about if or how your school will use social media. Point out some amazing things that are happening and evaluate if anyone outside of the school really knows about them. And it won't hurt to note that social media is a very inexpensive and extremely effective tool.

When you receive the green light to use social media, determine your target audience and ask what types of social media its members use in order to choose appropriate social media platforms. As we write this book, we are willing to bet the majority use Facebook, but that may change as new types of social media emerge. The key to success? Go where your audience is. If you force people to use a platform they do not use, they will not be engaged and your communication plan will not succeed. If you go where they are—Facebook, YouTube, Instagram, or others—your story *will* be heard and you *will* begin to hear more positive things about your school and district.

It is very refreshing to actually see the impact you're having on students' lives on a daily basis. It is exciting to know that when you post a positive message on Instagram in the morning, many students will be encouraged by you the moment they wake up or the instant they board the bus. It is fantastic to be able to use the power of social media to allow parents to see and share in the fun of their children's field trips, even if they are hundreds of miles away. And every time you tap into that power to encourage, share, engage, or connect, you reaffirm to your entire community that social media tools are beneficial—even necessary for schools today.

Social media is a part of our world. Take a moment and think about how often you see someone's Twitter handle or name on a social media site. Our job is to continue to ensure that our students become the most well-rounded people they can be. Today, a component of that job is educating them about social media and how they can use it to enhance their educational journey, as well as their life, professionally and socially.

Your Story Matters

Why did we write this book? To be honest, we are both educators who are tired of hearing the constant rhetoric of how poor education is. We grew tired of hearing how teachers are perceived as the bad guys, and tired of accusations against the laziness of this next generation. We work with amazing educators *every* day. We work with amazing kids *every* day. We have stories that are absolutely worth sharing. We realize it is time for us (and our communities) to focus on what is *right*

Join us in talking about and sharing what is right about education.

about schools. Social media empowers us all to do that. We hope you will join us in talking about and sharing what is *right* about education. Your story matters! Hop aboard and set sail on this journey. We look forward to hearing each and every story!

Stay connected at
YourSchoolRocks.com

Bibliography

Chapter One: The Power to Connect

1. Bob Dylan, "The Times They Are a-Changin'," *The Times They Are a-Changin'*, (Columbia Records, New York) 1964.

Chapter Three: iMovie Trailers

1. Dave Burgess, *Teach Like a PIRATE,* (San Diego: Dave Burgess Consulting, Inc., 2012).

Chapter Five: Facebook

1. Maeve Duggan, Amanda Lenhart, Cliff Lampe, and Nicole B. Ellison, "Parents and Social Media," July 16, 2015, http://www.pewinternet.org/2015/07/16/parents-and-social-media/.
2. Amanda Lenhart, "Teens, Social Media & Technology Overview 2015," April 9, 2015, http://www.pewinternet.org/2015/04/09/teens-social-media-technology-2015/.

Chapter Eight: Instagram Photos

1. Maeve Duggan, Nicole B. Ellison, Cliff Lampe, Amanda Lenhart, and Mary Madden, "Social Media Update 2014," *PewResearchCenter Internet, Science, & Tech*, January 9, 2015, http://www.pewinternet.org/ 2015/01/09/ social-media-update-2014/.

Chapter 16: Bringing It all Together

1. Gilad Bechar, "In With the Old: Mobile Marketing for Seniors," *Entrepreneur.com,* September 28, 2015, http://www.entrepreneur.com/article/250550.
2. Dave Burgess, *Teach Like a PIRATE* (San Diego: Dave Burgess Consulting, Inc., 2012).

Acknowledgments

Ryan McLane

I would like to express my gratitude to the following people who played a key role in my journey to create this book:

My wife Kristen, for her willingness to allow me to put the amount of hours I do into my job and the amount of time I spent on this book and without batting an eye.

My children, Molly and Macie, for always sharing me with 540 other kids.

My parents, Robert and Janet, for encouraging me, being hard on me, and knowing good things would happen.

Erin Casey and her amazing editing and production team. At times, she made me feel as though I were back in tenth-grade English class, but I appreciate her ability to make my words match what I was truly trying to say.

Dave and Shelley Burgess, for taking a chance on two unknown educators and passionately telling us, "We want to publish your book."

My former and current colleagues in education, even though there are too many to name individually, but I have learned so much from all of you.

Finally, to the countless number of students I have had the honor to work with over the past seventeen years, I can only hope that I have impacted you the way so many have impacted me.

Eric Lowe

I would like to express my heartfelt thanks to the following people who were instrumental in my journey to create this book:

My wife Sarah, for her passion and desire for education along with life, which always keeps pushing me to have a growth mindset. Thanks for always challenging me.

The students and educators at Beaver Local and specifically BLMS who have joined in on so many adventures with me and made our school a great place to be. The impact that you have made on me goes beyond words and is one I am so thankful for.

My colleagues at West Point Elementary, and the many others at Beaver Local and beyond, thanks for your friendship and investment in this great profession which enables us to make a difference.

My parents, Ed and Maria, for always demonstrating the importance of hard work and for investing themselves in me so that I could carry that same investment on to others.

Erin Casey and her team. It is remarkable to see how someone can transform the written word to look completely different, while maintaining the meaning behind those words.

Dave and Shelley Burgess, along with Ryan McLane, for inviting me to join in on this book, which I had never thought of as a possibility in my life. Thank you for providing an opportunity to tell our story, and thanks for the impact you have made on me.

More from

DAVE BURGESS Consulting, Inc.

Teach Like a PIRATE

Increase Student Engagement, Boost Your Creativity, and Transform Your Life as an Educator

By Dave Burgess (@BurgessDave)

Teach Like a PIRATE is the *New York Times*' best-selling book that has sparked a worldwide educational revolution. It is part inspirational manifesto that ignites passion for the profession, and part practical road map filled with dynamic strategies to dramatically increase student engagement. Translated into multiple languages, its message resonates with educators who want to design outrageously creative lessons and transform school into a life-changing experience for students.

P is for PIRATE

Inspirational ABC's for Educators
By Dave and Shelley Burgess
(@Burgess_Shelley)

Teaching is an adventure that stretches the imagination and calls for creativity every day! In *P is for Pirate*, husband and wife team Dave and Shelley Burgess encourage and inspire educators to make their classrooms fun and exciting places to learn. Tapping into years of personal experience and drawing on the insights of more than seventy educators, the authors offer a wealth of ideas for making learning and teaching more fulfilling than ever before.

Ditch That Textbook

Free Your Teaching and
Revolutionize Your Classroom
By Matt Miller (@jmattmiller)

Textbooks are symbols of centuries-old education. They're often outdated as soon as they hit students' desks. Acting "by the textbook" implies compliance and a lack of creativity. It's time to ditch those textbooks—and those textbook assumptions about learning! In *Ditch That Textbook*, teacher and blogger Matt Miller encourages educators to throw out meaningless, pedestrian teaching and learning practices. He empowers them to evolve and improve on old, standard teaching methods. *Ditch That Textbook* is a support system, toolbox, and manifesto to help educators free their teaching and revolutionize their classrooms.

Learn Like a PIRATE

Empower Your Students to
Collaborate, Lead, and Succeed
By Paul Solarz (@PaulSolarz)

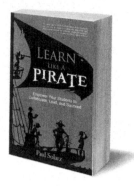

Today's job market demands that students be prepared to take responsibility for their lives and careers. We do them a disservice if we teach them how to earn passing grades without equipping them to take charge of their education. In *Learn Like a Pirate*, Paul Solarz explains how to design classroom experiences that encourage students to take risks and explore their passions in a stimulating, motivating, and supportive environment where improvement—rather than grades—is the focus. Discover how student-led classrooms help students thrive and develop into self-directed, confident citizens who are capable of making smart, responsible decisions, all on their own.

Pure Genius

Building a Culture of Innovation and
Taking 20% Time to the Next Level
By Don Wettrick (@DonWettrick)

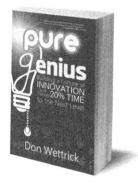

For far too long, schools have been bastions of boredom, killers of creativity, and way too comfortable with compliance and conformity. In *Pure Genius*, Don Wettrick explains how collaboration—with experts, students, and other educators—can help you create interesting, and even life-changing, opportunities for learning. Wettrick's book inspires and equips educators with a systematic blueprint for teaching innovation in any school.

50 Things You Can Do with Google Classroom
By Alice Keeler and Libbi Miller

It can be challenging to add new technology to the classroom, but it's a must if students are going to be well-equipped for the future. Alice Keeler and Libbi Miller shorten the learning curve by providing a thorough overview of the Google Classroom App. Part of Google Apps for Education (GAFE), Google Classroom was specifically designed to help teachers save time by streamlining the process of going digital. Complete with screenshots, *50 Things You Can Do with Google Classroom* provides ideas and step-by-step instructions to help teachers implement this powerful tool.

Master the Media
How Teaching Media Literacy Can Save Our Plugged-in World
By Julie Smith

Written to help teachers and parents educate the next generation, *Master the Media* explains the history, purpose, and messages behind the media. The point isn't to get kids to unplug; it's to help them make informed choices, understand the difference between truth and lies, and discern perception from reality. Critical thinking leads to smarter decisions—and it's why media literacy can save the world.

The Zen Teacher
Creating Focus, Simplicity, and Tranquility in the Classroom
By Dan Tricarico

Teachers have incredible power to influence, even improve, the future. In *The Zen Teacher,* educator, blogger, and speaker Dan Tricarico provides practical, easy-to-use techniques to help teachers be their best—unrushed and fully focused—so they can maximize their performance and improve their quality of life. In this introductory guide, Dan Tricarico explains what it means to develop a Zen practice—something that has nothing to do with religion and everything to do with your ability to thrive in the classroom.

The Innovator's Mindset
Empower Learning, Unleash Talent, and Lead a Culture of Creativity
By George Couros

The traditional system of education requires students to hold their questions and compliantly stick to the scheduled curriculum. But our job as educators is to provide new and better opportunities for our students. It's time to recognize that compliance doesn't foster innovation, encourage critical thinking, or inspire creativity—and those are the skills our students need to succeed. In The Innovator's Mindset, George Couros encourages teachers and administrators to empower their learners to wonder, to explore—and to become forward-thinking leaders.

About the Authors

Ryan McLane is the principal of Big Walnut Intermediate School, located in Sunbury, Ohio. He is passionate about making school about learning and fun and about sharing those great concepts with the community.

Ryan began his career as a high school social studies and business teacher, where he taught for twelve years and coached football and wrestling before making the transition to administration. He is a graduate of Muskingum College and Xavier University.

Ryan lives just outside of Columbus, Ohio, with his wife and two daughters.

 @McLane_Ryan

Eric Lowe is the principal of Beaver Local Middle School located in East Liverpool, Ohio. He began his career as an elementary teacher, where he taught for ten years while coaching baseball. He has served as the district athletic director for the past nine years and been involved in administration for the past six years. Eric is a graduate of Kent State University and Youngstown State University.

He is passionate about making school about learning and fun, while promoting the positives that go on in our schools. He also feels strongly that we must view the world of education with optimistic glasses in order to enable us to push others to reach their maximum potential. Eric lives in East Liverpool, Ohio, with his wife Sarah.

 @EricLowe21

CPSIA information can be obtained at www.ICGtesting.com
Printed in the USA
BVOW06s2024090916

461661BV00006B/55/P